Tell It Like It Is

YOU CAN'T MAKE THIS STUFF UP

Best wishes

LYN CLARKE

Lyn Clarke

Clarke Books
Anna Maria Island, Florida

Tell It Like It Is

YOU CAN'T MAKE THIS STUFF UP

CHAPTER ONE

Resurrecting Rodrigues

I have been a fan of music since the age of thirteen when, back in Wales, my sister and I used to dance to the early Rock & Roll songs played on the radio. At nineteen, encouraged by the sounds of the new Mersey Beat music explosion, I moved to live up in the Liverpool region. This was an amazing time of my life in which I made a good many friends and had exceptional times and happy memories. At the age of thirty six I had the fortuitous option to move to the USA and work in the Detroit area. Again, this time being encouraged by the new Motown Sound, I jumped at the chance and once again this momentous decision proved to be exciting and afforded me many memorable experiences and a cluster of stalwart new pals. At my present time of life I thought that I had heard it all and it was virtually impossible to replicate my passed musical excursions but I was wrong. In spite of all these positive musical related experiences nothing has move me, emotionally, as deep as the extremely riveting story of Sixto Dias Rodrigues.

At my home, on the Gulf of Mexico, Florida, one night my wife and I were searching for something interesting to watch on the television. She was scrolling down through a miriad of programs when we notice a documentary called "Searching for Sugar Man." The blurb stated that this film had recently won an Oscar for the Best Short Film which piqued our interest. The film lasted around an hour and it was so absorbing that my wife and I did not speak a single word during the entire program. When the film finished we eagerly began to chat about this most unusual depiction of a bizarre set of circumstances and the re-sounding victory which the musician Rodrigues, the sincere subject of the story, eventually found in later life. This singer/ song writer, went from relative success to absolute rejection and abject poverty where he literally disappeared from the face of the earth. Some thirty years later he was rediscovered, through some amazing detective work initiated by an almost unknown, yet inquisitive, South African music lover. This eventual chanced intervention would put our hero back on the road to fame and good fortune where he so rightly belonged.

Back in 1968 this shy young man, from down town Detroit, launched his career with a compilation of songs entitled "Cold Fact." Such tracks as "Sugar Man", "Inner City Blues", "Cruci-fy Your Mind" and "I Wonder" were rich in soul with amazing lyrics. In 1971 he followed this up with his second venture entitle "Coming from Reality", again with earthy tracks such as "Street Boy", "Can't Get Away", "I Think of You", "I'll Slip Away" and "Silver Words." Rodrigues, singing in a style not unlike Bob Dylan but with a much more melodic tone, began what seemed to be a highly successful musical endeavor. To everyone, con-nected with both recordings in this venture, it seemed certain to be every bit a success with massive hits but for some unknown reason sales did not take off. Perhaps it was simply a question of bad timing what with the war in Vietnam, the anti-war demon-strations and the race riots in Detroit. Maybe people, at that time, just did not want to hear the down to earth messages of his lyr-ics like "I lost my job two weeks before Christmas". Whatever the reason after about a year his record production company dropped him and to all extent of purposes that was the end of his musical career. Sixto went back to playing in the local bars like The Bronx, The Old Miami, The Sewer and the Motor City Brewing Company, in and around Cass Avenue, once again for little or no money at all.

However, unknown to everyone concerned, fate took a hand when a young lady from America went to visit her boyfriend in South Africa, during the Apartheid Era, and took a copy of Rodrigues' music with her. This serendipitous event re-launched his fortunes as his music was avidly taken up, by the mainly white youths of that time, almost as their themes for the Anti Apartheid movement. Soon bootleg copies of his music were being sold, on the black market, as the word concerning this new unconventional style of music, caused his popularity to increase and spread. Virtually every young people's party, in those days, played his music and as the word circulated he became the new poet that expressed their current emotions and beliefs. When Apartheid was eventually and soundly defeated and the years rolled on Rodrigues' music became a symbol of this victory and then sales , through now legal channels, really took off. He now sold more records in this market than either Elvis or The Beatles which rocketed him from an American Zero to now being a South African Hero. While all this was going on Rodrigues, unaware of these facts, carried on with his humble life in the working class areas of the Motor City in Michigan, USA.

Through these twenty or so years Big Sky, the holding company who represented his business interests in South Africa, religiously sent all his royalty checks to the owner of his previous, now defunked , Sussex Record in California. However, Rodrigues never received one red cent and therefore had absolutely no idea that his music was so popular in another part of the world. The mystery thickened when for years it was rumored, throughout his adoring fan base, that he had become so dejected by his lack of success that he had consequently and tragically taken his own life. A South African music guru, Stephen Segerman , coincidently nick named Sugar Man, wrote the foot notes on Rodrigues' record releases. He summed these up by saying that there was absolutely no information concerning the existence or location of this reclusive man. This caught the eye of Greg Batholamew, a South African news reporter, who took up the challenge and was determined to find out the truth behind the whole inexplicable chain of events. He set out to get the real story and thus put all speculations to rest. After several frustrating years he finally found the location of one of Rodrigues' three daughters and after a long telephone conversation she told him that her father was alive and still living a humble life in Detroit. She gave him a telephone number to call and when he did the voice at the other end of the line was unmistakably that of the long lost Rodrigues. He told the downtrodden musician that for all these many years he had been revered in South Africa and that his reputation was immense. He also said that his music was the anthems that had inspired the youth of South Africa to rise up and beat Apartheid. It took a great deal of convincing that this was not a prank but finally the he persuaded Rodrigues that it was all very true. Bartholamew flew to Detroit and after a protracted face to face meeting he persuaded the singer to go to South Africa and witness this phenomenon for himself.

A six concert tour was arranged which immediately sold out with crowds averaging fifty thousand people. When he arrived at the airport in South Africa this humble man stood on the side walk not realizing that the limo parked at the curb was waiting for him. The concerts were highly emotional as the fans witnessed their hero literally come back to life. Many were in a complete emotional state sobbing with tears of joy. They could not comprehend that their long lost idol had been found to rise from the ashes of mediocrity. At each concert there was a ten minute welcoming ovation where the fans went hysterical as they could not believe what they were witnessing. Rodrigues countered by thanking them for keeping him alive which brought on more frantic cheering and terms of long lost endearments. As he sang his songs the crowd join in knowing each and every last word and the emotional meeting of the fans, with the man they thought had been lost forever, came to a fairy tale ending. At last Rodrigues is now reaping the financial rewards which he should have been paid during all those years of poverty. He has given almost all of his new found wealth to his family and friends and still lives a humble life in the same run down house in a run down area of Detroit. He still chops up fire wood to feed the cast iron pot bellied stove which heats his living room. He still walks around his neighborhood, in wind, rain or snow, and he still can be found playing in the local bars for next to nothing. What a lesson in humility for us all to learn as it is the attitude, which we hold in life, that is of prime importance and that we must pass these on to teach and inspire others. He held on to his resolve and belief, in his own abilities, and never ever gave up or gave in when all around was gloom and doom.

On my last visit to the south west area of Detroit I went to Dearborn Records and bought both of Rodrigues' afore mention C. D's. I play them often and now I too have become a huge fan of this humble man. Detroit city is currently going through some tough times but with such honest and inspiring people, like Rodrigues, this once vibrant city will rise again. In days gone by I have met The Beatles, Rod Stewart, Elton John, The Who and The Rolling Stones but this man's grit inspires me. Rodrigues, the man that never lost faith when all his music hopes were dashed, remained strong of heart. He bore his humble life with acceptance and every challenge as an obstacle for inspiration. In his own inimitable words "I'll thank you for your time and you'll thank me for mine." He is also noted as saying that "Music unlocks our inhibitions and lyrics set us free."

N.B. I have just had an epiphany. I remembered that back in the late 1970's, as Road Manager for a Bay City band called The Burdens, I arranged a gig for them at the Old Miami in Detroit. After their set a quiet, unassuming man came over and casually chatted with us for a while. I have just realized this man was Rodrigues himself. Wow!

CHAPTER TWO

Cometh The Hour, Cometh The Man

I n this day and age, of self absorbed people, it is a rare privilage to meet anyone with their feet planted firmly on the ground. Most of today's people cannot go fifteen minutes without refering to their I-pads, smart phones or computers and it seems that the age of instant gratification has gone amok. Therefore, when a person comes into one's life that considers this most disconcert trend as being redundant, to the extreme, it is a breath of fresh air. The art of a long, one on one, protracted and meaningful conversations is a diminishing quality but when a person has the knack of riveting your attention this is an experience not to be missed. I am sure there have been others in the past who possessed this ability, such as the Dalai Lama or Mahatma Gandy but few mere mortals had the opportunity to have met them. However, I have been fortunate to meet Paul "Ace" Hayward, a man who cared so much about other people that he would donate his time and advice to virtually anyone he happened to meet. His positive words of encouragement and his views on life were free for anyone who cared to take the time and listen.

I moved from the Detroit area of Michigan to the fabulous island of Anna Maria, Florida back in 1999. It was a pivotal decision in my life and, as good fortune would have it, this turned out to be the absolute best decision of my entire existence. I had two years of work left before I could take my long awaited early retirement and being able to do this in a tropical paradise was, to say the least, amazing. In my earlier life I had been a rugby player for twenty five years in Wales and England before emigrating to America. I was soon recruited , at an Irish bar, by a bunch of Brits to join their soccer team. They were a feisty bunch of English, Scottish, Irish and Welsh working class guys but, when it came to soccer, they knew their stuff. We played respectively in the Detroit League, the Great Lakes League and The Michigan United League and did considerably well in all three. On coming south I played kick around soccer for a couple of years in Manatee County then I hung up my boots. About five years later I was sitting on the beach, having a cocktail with my wife and watching an astonishing sun set, when Tim Tedesco happened to pass by. He asked me if I would consider kicking the ball around, in a not too serious manner, on a Sunday evening with a bunch of local guys. I told him that I had not kicked a soccer ball around for quite some time and might be a little rusty but he was most convincing. A few days later I was there and for about two months my legs were so stiff and sore that they felt like lead. About two years later our group was approached by AMICC and asked to start an Island League which was formed with eight teams and extra players on a waiting list hoping to join. Good players came out of the woodwork, from as far away as Bradenton, Palmetto and Sarasota, to sign up for these highly competitive games.

It was around this time that I first met Paul Hayward who was a Canadian that lived, ate and breathed soccer. He had a distinguished soccer playing careers at youth, college and proffessional levels. He had been a soccer coach, adviser, mentor and a motivator to many budding soccer stars. He turned up, out of the blue, and after a short span of time the other players were attentively listening to every word of his very sage advice. To make the league more interesting, each year all the players were reselected to form new teams as the mixture of talent was redistributed. No matter which team Paul Hayward ended up on he immediately took over the reins. He was a wizard at quickly assessing each player in his squad and, by advising them as to the best position for them to play, his teams always did well. The second season into the league, to no-one's surprise, his team won the Challenge Cup. I never had the pleasure of playing on a team with him but from the opposite side of the field I admired his astute play and the on field advise he constantly gave to his lesser talented players. Paul had nicknames for virtually everyone he liked, such as Speedy, Puff Daddy, Spanky, Plugger and Dirty Little Bastard, and these were taken as compliments by those privileged enough to be so called. He not only advised the players he also advised the referees and even the organizing league officials. Because the games were seven verses seven , on a full sized field, he instigated the no off-side rule which made the games faster, higher scoring and more exciting. Throughout all of these activities most people did not know that Paul had been battling cancer for several years. His original cancer was in remission but during the time, that I am now refering to, it had returned with a vengeance. He played on but there were weeks when he would quietly disappear and go into hospital for treatment.

He rarely told anyone that he was going or mentioned the traumatic event when he returned. I was sitting at home one day when my phone rang. It was Paul asking if I could give him a lift. Thinking that he was at his condo I said "Sure, I'll be right over." He said "I'm not at home, I'm at Moffitt Hospital on the north side of Tampa about an hour and a half away." My wife and I drove up there and I went into the reception area to inquire as to his where abouts but they could not locate him. As all this confusion ensued I looked up and here he comes sauntering down the hallway with a big smile on his face. When we arrived back at his place I had to assist him up the stairs, leading to his condo, where he flopped onto the bed and went to sleep. A week later he was back up at the soccer field and a further week after he was playing again. To the best of my knowledge, three times the hospital gave him a month to live and three times he showed up back at the soccer fields on game night. This is the way it went and rarely ever did I hear one word of complaint concerning what most people would consider to be a most cruel twist of fate. He was a man amongst men.

I never knew Paul when he was growing up but somewhere, someone instilled an amazing deep sense of sincerity and compassion into this individual. Right up to the end of his life he still took time to advise others on how to overcome their problems and troubles of life. One of the last things that I remember him saying to me, probably brought on by the finality of his predicament, was "Don't sweat the small stuff." The last time I saw him was at last years Cup Final when my team was beaten 4 goals to 2. I had a bad chest infection and I felt my contribution to that game was not what it should have been. I was feeling a little despondent but, in the bar afterward, Paul looked over at me raised his thumb and smiled. At this point in time he was quite frail and because of my potentially infectious condition, I was unable to approach him in his delicate state of health. I shouted to him, across the bar, that he owed me a hug which I expected to get when my ailment was cured. Unfortunately, I never saw him again but I will get my hug one day, of that I am sure. I can only hope that when the time comes, for me to meet my maker, I can face the situation with the same stoic resolve as that displayed by Hayward The Brave. In his own inimitable style he has shown us how to be resolute in the face of over whelming odds. Now that he is no longer with us, we still have the happy memories of his broad smile, barrel chest, curly blonde mop of hair and his always kind words.

So there it is. He was a person who had the precious gift of the ability to inspire others. Meeting Paul Hayward has given me a new belief that there have been others, of his kind, who also roamed this earth and made significant changes to peoples lives on and off the field of play. Not only that, special people have the inert way of making indelible and lasting impression as they go through life. Paul Hayward was one of these and he has done this for me and I thank him for his time and sincerely kind words. I am some twenty years older than him and he said to me, one day, that he wish that he could have my life. When I asked why he said "Because I could have twenty more years with Jackson Kai," the son that he adored. The son that, I feel, kept him going for two or three more years than the experts predicted. On the beach, at the Sand Bar, we all gathered in a large circle to remember this remarkable man. People from Canada, Vermont, West Virginia and Florida all brought together having been touched by this unique person. As the assembly was breaking up it began to rain so we retired to the outdoor restaurant canopy for shelter. Although it was now pouring down the sun was still setting. This was to me a unique sight with the large, bright and clear sun setting behind the falling rain. It reminded me of the line in a Glen Campbell song "I want to go where the sun is shining, through the pouring rain." As I made a comment about this phenomenon a lady, who I had never met before, was standing next to me and she turned, stared straight at me and said "Hayward." A large, bright and clear sun shining through the gloom of life. A life which can sometimes be an uncertain and often perilously journey. Incidentally, he and I really enjoyed Jerry Seinfeld and we often discussed this series and in particular the zany antics of the quirky Kramer character. I always had the knack of making him smile and I remember one day when we were watching a soccer game together. The goal keeper, of one particular team, was beaten all ends up but luckily for him the ball rebounded off the post. I looked at Paul and said "The father, the son and the goalie post." I thought he was going to bust a gut and I can still envisage his broad smile as he chuckled uncontrollably. He really enjoyed this style of quirky wit and incidents, like this, amused him immensely. God willing we will all meet him again, one day, at that far post.

Since Paul has passed on I found myself browsing around at a Goodwill resale store one day looking for nothing in particular but anything in general. I was in the sports area just looking for something that I could not live without but I never know exactly what that is until I find it. For some inexplicable reason I found myself standing in front of a scattered pile of woolen knitted scull caps. I say this because I hardly ever wear caps or hats of any sort and the temperature outside was almost ninety degrees. I have no idea what prompted me to begin rummaging through them but there, right at the bottom of the pile, was a Eleven Man Gang knitted cap. I had one of those spine chilling sensation up and down my back as I stood there holding the cap and I knew that it was Paul just saying "Hello". I naturally bought the cap, without a second thought, not even knowing when if ever I would wear it. However, a month or so later, on the spur of the moment, I arrange a long overdue trip to the Shetland Islands which is way up in the North Atlantic between Norway and Iceland. Unfortunately, while there, I somehow lost that cap on one of the crazy nights while cementing the bond of Anglo/American good will. The good news is that some hapless rapscallion is now, most probably, wearing Hayward's cap under his horned Viking head piece. Perhaps some of Hayward's charisma will rub off on this person and the cap will bring , that unknown islander, a modicum of sensibility. I am not a devoutly religious person but I have experienced some strangely unexplainable events. This leads me to believe that there is a connection, what ever it is, between us and our loved ones on the other side. From the other side he has helped me to accept this little known fact and I now feel secure in the knowledge that he will

17

be carefully watching over us all. Incidentally, our island soccer Challenge Cup now proudly bears his name.

As a side bar, here's a thought that would amuse Ace. The other day I heard someone refer to "a pint of strawberries." How can a solid object be measured by a liquid volume? A thought provoking enigma wrapped up in an riddle, surrounded by a mystery!

CHAPTER THREE
Vikings Are Cooler Than Pirates

I have just returned from a four week whirl wind visit to Wales, England and Scotland. I took eight individual flights and slept in ten different beds and visited dozens of different cities, towns and villages. During this time I met many old friends and made new acquaintances, too many to mention. With my son Richard and daughter Louise I attended the wedding, in Cardiff, of my niece Jemma. I explored the Somerset towns of Wells, Cheddar and Glastonbury where I climbed to the top of its world famous Tor. It is said after his much reported visit to Ireland that Saint Patrick resided here, until his death. At the top of this steep hill I met a group of ladies, all standing in a circle, while singing songs of encouragement. I found out later that they were all cancer survivers on a cleansing retreat and moral boosting pilgrimage. At Wells, the view out of my hotel bedroom window was straight across "The Green" towards the extremely impressive front of its amazing cathedral. Not the biggest in the Christian world but by far one of the most intricately ornamented facades that I have ever witnessed. I had to visit Cheddar, if for no other reason but the fact that it has given, to the world, its very own famous cheese which has been widely reproduced all over this planet.

At my home town of Pontypool I sold my various books in the high street and made many new friends. While there also I was invited, by my old rugby playing buddies, to a gentleman's dinner with the guest speaker being none other than the number one referee of that illustrious sport, Nigel Owen. This event was hosted by Brynmawr Rugby Club and was excellently organized in every possible manner. My father, as a young man fresh out of the Monmouth Haberdasher's School, played for this club and so I promised the Club's Chairman that I would sent a photo, recording that time, to him. This, he promised me, would be put on display for all club members to see. Up in Port Sunlight, at the Bridge Hotel, I had a great night with my rugby buddies from that colorful era of my life. The night was filled with stories, jokes and laughter enhanced by some very fine English ales. A notable day was spent shopping at Chester, one of my all time favorite cities, with my wife and daughter. I also took the opportunity to visit several betting shops where I was able to place bets on various horse races. All these occasions were fabulous but the highlight of the entire trip was when my son and I flew up to the Shetland Isles for what was to prove to be, a momentous time. The fact that it was the weekend of Father's Day and also the longest day of the year, where the sun only went down for three hours, just added to this unique and adventurous episode.

Richard and I met at Manchester Airport at 7-30 AM on Thursday 19th June. He had to get a 5-00 AM train from Doncaster while I was driven down from the Burnley area by my daughter, Louise. From there we had a 9-00 AM flight to Inverness, on the main land of Scotland, where we arrived around two hours later. We then had a five hour lay over while waiting for our Shetland flight which we found out, much to our surprise, was also calling at the Orkney Isles on the way up. At Inverness we took a bus down town where we shopped, had muscles for lunch and played a few free games of pool before returning to the airport. After a quick stop at the Orkneys we hopped on over to the Shetlands which, for the uninitiated, is about halfway between Norway and Iceland. Except for a skiing trip in Sweden, back in the late 1960's, this is the farthest north that I have ever been on this planet. Since my trip originated in Florida, the temperature differential was about 40 degrees Farhenheit and the terrain had changed from subtropical to near frozen tundra with hardly a tree in sight. We hired a taxi to take us from the airport into Lerwick, the capital of these isolated lands, which is around thirty miles north from the southern most tip of these desolate and barren group of island. We arrived at our lodgings, the Fort Charlotte House, at around 10 PM and after a quick respite we headed out on the town to get the lay of the land. We found a lively bar but we were told that there would be no music entertainment on this particular night. However, within around half an hour, out of nowhere, we heard some highly energetic noises coming from the upstairs room. We immediately followed the pounding beat to find a bunch of young Norwegian men, who had arrived by yacht that very afternoon, hamming it up to beat the band. The one was playing the piano in a Norse come Celtic mixture of sound that was different yet boldly exciting. His friends then followed suite by taking down instruments, which were hanging on a nearby wall, quickly tuned them and proceeded to accompany him on bango, violin and accordian. The whole event turned out to be a totally unrehearsed yet unforgettable sequence of music. During the quiet intervals we each shared our own individual stories as to why we had come to Lerwick on this particular weekend. Our new Norwegian friends were all art students and had sailed over from Bergen, to set up an Art Exhibition which they were to display at the local museum. We, on the other hand, had a much more sinister reason for being there as we were on a mission to find out the intricate details of how and why my father had died.

We slept well that night which was unusual because at this latitude it was only dark from around mid-night to 3-00 AM. In the morning, after a wonderful three course breakfast, we were off to the museum to study the archives concerning the infamous explosion in Lerwick harbor circa November 22nd 1943. Everyone there was most pleasant and helpful as we toured the World War II displays of how that tragic engagement had affected these islands and its stoic people. We paid particular interest to the information on the intrepid Shetland Bus stories as, bringing Nowegian people away from Nazi oppression, was all part and parcel of what my father was involved in doing. His boat, however, did not carry refugees but was there to protect the ships that were involved in this perilous enterprise. My father was an ordinary British sailor vicariously involve in an extra-ordinary set of circumstances. His boat MTB 686, was one of many such light weight speedy crafts that ran the gauntlet of danger across the cold and cruel North Sea in what can only be described as extremely dangerous conditions. The weather and the turbulent sea was enough to contend with but these boats had to avoid floating mines and the German battle ships which were out there specifically to intercept them.

The three main missions this floatilla of craft had was [1] To locate any enemy battle ships as they attempted to reach Norway from the North Atlantic Sea. [2] To bring back precision ball bearings, from Sweden, needed for military plane, ship and tank revolving gun turrets, and [3] To pick up and bring back, to the Shetlands, Norwegian civilians who then would be trained as spies and eventually be taken back to Norway to ply their talents. However, these spies were intentionally misinformed that the Allies intention was to invade Norway instead of Normandy. When D-Day finally arrived 250,000 German troops were guarding Norway and were kept away from the intended invasion sites on the French Normandy beaches. These were harrowing night trips and the toll could be seen in my father's face on a photograph which was taken a week or so before his demize. The other disturbing factor was that on these trips they had to carry mines, torpedoes and extra aviation fuel, on the top deck, in those choppy waters and just one mistake could cause the whole lot to explode and take the frail boat with them. The life expectation of an motor torpedo boat was six months from the time that it was launched and therefore to say that these trips were perilous is a gross under statement. Sometimes four of these boats would make the trip across to Norway only to see just two of them return. The sailors, on the surviving two boats, would have witness the sinking of their friends knowing well that this could happen to them on a similar trip at a later date.

One day when my father's boat was being readied, for that particular nights operation, there was an enormous explosion which blew it right out of the water. All of the crew of MTB 686 were either instantly killed or died in the following days from their extensive burns. It is difficult to get any concrete information on the cause of this hapless disaster. The War Department will not release the actual details to prevent the blame being laid on any one person. I have gathered information saying that a shot was mistakenly fired by the gunner who was preparing the cannon. Alternatively, I have read another version saying that two officers were trying to start a faulty engine which back fired and ignited the fumes from the highly volatile aviation fuel. There have also been whispers of covert sabotage as Germany had just as many spies on the Shetlands as we had in Norway. Whatever the cause, my father and seven other brave sailors died a horrible death that day. This was further amplified by the fact that the other moored British naval vessals were instructed to fire on the boat to sink it and prevent the flames spreading to the other tightly packed armada in the harbor. This is an added factor as to why the real facts have been sealed for all of the past seventy plus years. The people of Lerwick embraced my son and I when we explained the purpose of our visit to the Shetlands. One of the museum attendants, named Trevor, was so impressed with our endeavor that he volunteered to take us around the harbor, by rowing boat. This whole experience was surreal as he leisurely rowed us about the inlet while pointing out all the notable land marks and points of interest of the surrounding bay and town.

My son and I went back a second day and saw photos of the Lerwick Harbor after that massive explosion. The devastation was immense with buildings being leveled and windows and doors being blown out for hundreds of yards away. I also found out that some of these poor souls, from the explosion, were walking about completely engulfed in fire while the local people tried, in desperation, to douse the flames. It was one of the biggest explosions of that war , so much so, that it was recorded in a New York newspaper, of that time, as being an extraordinary news worthy event. My son and I also found out that those who died that day were buried in an old grave yard up in an area of Lerwick called the Knab. We had already visited the plaque, that was installed, around the year 2000, by a Shetland/Norwegian group, on which was listed all names of the eight sailors who died in that event. After a long cliff side walk we reached the cemetery which was huge and situated on the side of a steep hill which ran down to the shore. We started at the top and worked our way along each row of graves but found nothing of interest. Half way down the hill, towards the sea inlet, there was a wall. We were told, by a man walking his dog, that we had to look in the old, old section as we had merely been looking in the old section. Again we went along each row of graves and I was ready to quit but my son urged me on. Finally, in the very last line, the one nearest to the sea wall, we found what we were looking for, a line of four grave stones. We marked off, from our list, the three grave stones on which were the names and the date corresponding with the information on the harbor plaque. One of the other names on the plaque was that of a Norwegian sailor which now accounted for four. Next was a grave on which was etched the words "Two unknown sailors" dated 22/11/1943. So now we have six of the men who died that day but two were still unaccounted for. Is my father one of the two unknown sailors in the grave or is he one of the other two unfound sailors probably lying at the botton of the harbor? I will probably never know for certain.

I previously mentioned the tragic departure of my good soccer buddy Paul Hayward, who I considered a man amongst men. I never mentioned that at his funeral celebration, on the beach by the Sand Bar Restaurant, his sister gave each of us a pebble with the word PE.ACE. Yes it does say peace but after the dot is the name that we symbolically used for Paul "Ace" Hayward. I put my hand into my pocket and pulled out that very pebble which I had brought all the way from Florida. I would like to think that my father is one of the sailors in the unmarked grave and so I knelt down and placed that pebble at the foot of that unmarked head stone. There it will lie, hopefully undisturbed, for many years to come and I feel that it is symbolic of my two brave men who are now to be linked together in the exact same spot. Two of the people that, in my lifetime, I have greatly admired and I will never forget their presence on this earth. I find it fitting that my search for the truth has brought me to this exact geographical spot and at this time of my life. I now feel that I have accomplished my quest and although I am not without faults if there is one thing that I do possess, it is complete loyalty to the ones I love.

That night was the Summer Solstice, the longest day of the year and fortuitously in Lerwick there was a Viking Festival. Each region, on these far flung isles, has their own Viking group and this day is one of only two times in the whole year that they all converge in one place. The parade was fun with marauding gangs of Vikings rattling their shields and shouting veiled threats. However, the best sights were seeing these wild men around the town bars that night. In one bar I met and had a long conversation with one of the Viking group leaders. His outfit was totally impressive with real raven feathers woven into his helmet. He told me that before he volunteered to become a leader he already knew that his total uniform would cost him 10,000 British Pounds. The sold silver clasps, that held his cloak together , alone cost 1,000 BP's. This event gave me a bit of an insight into what being a Viking was all about. The fun was endless and I was happy to be a part of it. Where I live in Florida we have pirates, buccaneers and privateers but they are somewhat tame compared to a marauding band of fear instilling Vikings. They swig beer from hollowed out cow horns and wave around real swords and axes which they bang against their shields. In the harbor there is a three quarter scaled Viking ship which, at their winter gathering, they will burn with flaming torches to simulate a Viking leaders burial. Not unlike what had happened to my father back in 1943.

On our last day there my son and I hired a car and went over to Skalloway, the previous capitol city of the Shetlands, then on around the Mid Westland to such towns as Tingwall, Whiteness, Sandness and Saint Ninian's Island. We stopped at Walls and had the rare treat of eating lunch at the most northerly Fish and Chip shop in the United. Kingdom. The terrain, at this northern longitude, was mainly treeless but we did see numerous scatterings of wild Shetland ponies and these islands are known for the only place, on God's Green Earth, where you can see brown sheep. Yes, not white or black but brown. Basically we covered the lower half of these fascinating islands but did not get up as far north as the isles of Unst, Yell, Fetlar or the Outer Skerries where to get there you have to cross by car ferry. At the end of our tour, where we had witnessed wild seels, sea otters, puffins and numerous sea fowl, we then drove south to the airport and returned the hire car. After some tentative negotiations, with the airline, we then flew to Aberdeen where we stayed overnight. The next morning we went by taxi, at 5-00 AM, back to the airport for an early morning flight which landed us back at Manchester at 9-00 AM. Richard had to go to work that day and so as soon as we had cleared customs he took the early train back to Doncaster to pick up his car. My daughter Louise was there to wisk me back to her house, in Read, Lancashire, for two days of rest and relaxation before making the long trek back to my Florida home and almost perpetual sunshine.

It was an amazing experience, one which I will not soon forget. I feel that it was the right time, of my life, to undertake this arduous trip. At my age it is difficult to predict what the future might bring. I am hale and hearty now but who can forsee what ailments might beset me at a future date. In my circumstance it is better to face the past now , than allow Old Father Time to rob me of such a unique opportunity. Amen.

CHAPTER FOUR

The Arthurian Connection

Growing up, in my blue collar town of Pontypool, there wasn't much to do for entertainment and there was even less to be proud of. Back in those days, times were extremely hard for the working class man and apart from the pubs and workmen's clubs there was precious little for us to do but drink beer. However, one thing that kept us all going was the sport of rugby football and our home town team which was literally known, for its prowess, throughout the world. On home match days our town would be filled with a swarming crowd all sporting our colors of red, white and black on shirts, banners, flags and rosettes. The town was a hive of activity with the pub patrons spilling out into the narrow streets and all concerned were filled with the anticipation of what excitement was to come. A victory was expected and in nothing less than a spectacular manner. The droves of people flocked down to The Park from the town end and up from Pontymoil and even down the hills from Trevethin and Wainfelin. They all came together in one heaving mass both in the seated viewing stand and opposite on the natural embankment where the less afflu-ent supporters would congregate. After a rousing hour and a half of rugby they would troop out in all directions and eager-ly return to their favorite watering holes to relive what they had just witnessed. Now deliriously happy and loudly singing they would avidly drink their beers and boast about their be-loved Pontypool rugby team which they idolized and adored. On Sundays they would recuperate before the following Mon-day which saw them return to work in the surrounding coal mines, steel works and factories.

There was only one thing that could out do their unwaver-ing devotion for their home town team and that was their love for the Welsh national rugby team. Many a Pontypool player had the honor of being selected to represent his country and, for a Welshman, this was considered to be the holy grail of priz-es. On one occation I recall that there were no less than seven Pontyool men in one Welsh side of fifteen players and this high lighted just how staunch the men from my home town and local villages were. They were regarded as some of the most skillful, astute and physically tough men walking the planet and when they played for their country their pride and devotion took their dedication up another notch or two. These men played for their country, at the National Stadium, against such revered teams as New Zealand, Australia, South Africa, Argentina, all the home and European countries and all the Pacific Island countries at the highest level. Of course, they also played against all these same nations, away from home, which usually entailed a two to three month arduous tour which was long and strenuously demanding. As well as being selected for their country, on in-ternational duty, there was also another honor of being select-ed for a combined team of the four British countries which was aptly named the Barbarians. This team consisted of players from England, Wales, Scotland and Ireland and to be selected for this multi-national team was, in a way, even more prestigious than a national team. Here once more, Pontypool players have been duly honored. The match between the Barbarians and visitors was always the grand finale game for any touring side and was played, almost inevitably, at the famous Arms Park Stadium in the Welsh capital of Cardiff.

This preamble brings me to a cold and dreary Saturday, in Cardiff, on the 27th of January in 1973. Here I witnessed, what so many rugby fans have designated as, one of the sporting world's finest moments when the Barbarians team defeated the dreaded and almost invincible New Zealand "All Blacks." Every sport has its special moments and I have personally witnessed quite a few of them, in my time, but this day will forever be etched in my mind until the day I die. This Barbarians victory has captured the imagination and has been firmly entrenched in the realm of rugby football folk law for ever. For the sixty thousand or so rugby fans, who were fortunate enough to be in attendance, this was a rare and unexpected treat. The game was evenly matched when, mid way through the first half, a New Zealand player launched one of their stereotypical high up-and-under kicks deep into the home teams territory. The crowd gasped in anticipation because this tactic usually put the defending team under immense pressure. The ball was caught by a defending player, who immediately transferred it to Llanelli's mercurial runner Phil Bennett. Much to New Zealand's surprise and amazement instead of kicking for touch, to relieve the pressure , Bennett set off on a counter attacking run. This proved to be the catallyst which, in the twinkle of an eye, turned this momentous game on it's head and, at the same time created a unique historic event.

As he sprinted to the right of the pitch Bennett did three devastating side steps to elude the would be New Zealand defense. In the twinkle of an eye, this quickly changed direction of play which proceeded to go to his left. This completely caught the New Zealand players flat footed and totally off guard and at the same time it brought into play a whole slew of rampaging Barbarian players. In a scintillating manner the whole Barbarian team was now thundering down the left flank, of the field, in eager anticipation of becoming involved in the play. Their blood was up as they inter-passed in a fast and furious manner while galloping towards the enemy goal line. They looked like a charging herd of bulls as they furiously ran, with one goal in mind, to get to and cross their opponents goal line. The crowd now roaring their team on , in combined ecstasy, as from their vantage points they could see that the New Zealand team were in disarray. With twenty five yards to go one of the Barbarians slung the ball out wide to the waiting winger but before it could get to the intended target, in a flash and from seemingly nowhere, came the man of the moment, Gareth Edwards. It all happened at such great pace that the opponents were left flat footed as Gareth sprinted along the touch line and dived over and score near the corner flag. All the enemy saw of him was a clean pair of heels and the number on the back of his shirt. This whole sequence of events took less than one minute of real time and was absolutely surreal. The Barbarians were seventeen to zero ahead at half time and never lost the lead, for the entire game, and it virtually broke the backs of one of the finest rugby teams in the world. That emphatic win, of twenty three points to eleven gave the number one rated rugby team, in the entire world, a severe shock and sent them home to think again. A few years after this game three Pontypool players made rugby history by becoming the first complete front row ever to be chosen to represent Wales. Graham Price, Bobby Windsor and Charlie Faulkner were the players in question and our town could not be more proud than to have three of its favorite sons involved in top flight rugby games. Many Pontypool men have made their home town proud, far too many to mention, but it would be wrong not to name one, the enigmatic Ray Prosser. Pooler! Pooler! Pooler! As a side bar, for the people of Pontypool, they might just be interested to know there is a small town, on the outskirts of Savannah, Georgia in the USA named "Pooler." I kid you not. Check it out!

After this historic victory a rash of Celtic lore sprang forth which, over time, was amply embellished. From this singular piece of sporting history came the following, very unlikely, saga.

Two Welsh valley men went to Cardiff to see Wales play against England, their centuries old arch enemy. Between them they could only afford one ticket and so they tossed up a coin, outside the ground, to see which of them would go in. Dai won the toss and after entering the stadium he proceded right up to the top most back row of the terrace where he could see down into the street below. From there he gave his friend, Taffy, a blow by blow account of the events on the field. With prompt regularity the crowd would loudly groan and Dai would tell Taffy that yet another brave Welsh player had been injured and carried off the field of play. [this before substitutes were allowed.] Wales were now down to just one player, against the whole England team, when there was a tumultuous and deafening roar from the crowd. At this Taffy shouted up "What happened." to which Dai shouted down "Gareth scored!"

Such was the esteem, charisma and mystique that these amazing sportsmen were held in for years to come. With Phil Bennett, Gareth Edwards, JPR Williams, Gerald Davies, John Dawes and Mervyn Davis being involved, just under half of that victorious Barbarians team were Welshmen. Those were the halcien days with stories of glory, bravery and almost unbelievable skills that literally stunned opponents and left them demoralized. Back then the game was an amateur status sport and we were taught in all the skills of how best to evade the enemy defenders. Today the game is a professional sport where the tactics entails deliberate direct contact and constant regurgitation of the ball from loose mauls. The scrums today are dictated by so many minor rules that it quite often takes five minutes, of laborious repeats, before it can be successfully completed to the referees satisfaction. In my day the game was free flowing with plenty of open running and inter-passing whereas today it is rigidly structured and, far too often, highly predictable. It is almost as if the spontaneity has been coached out of all the players and everyone is molded into the same boring pattern. I didn't think that I would ever say this but right now the Rugby League code, of this game, is more exciting to watch. It will be a cold day in hell before we ever again witness such a spectacular game or see a try the likes of which occurred on that auspicious day in 1973. In days of yore there were many stories about the bravery of such Celtic characters as King Arthur, Sir Galahad and Sir Lancelot. Other stories, from that historic era, concern the wizardry of Merlin the Magician. Now, in the modern annuls of time, there is another beloved Welsh son of equal stature. Sir Gareth of Cardiff, the man who has been honored for his many heroic deeds and for once again making the entire nation of Wales eternally proud.

CHAPTER FIVE

This 'Ole Heart Of Mine
(Has Beat A Million Times)

From as early as I can remember I have been a runner. I grew up poor and consequently our family never owned a car and I never had a bicycle. To hang out with those friends of mine, that had bicycles, I ran beside of them as they pedaled. As we chatted they would ride for miles with me jogging along just like a faithful dog. I accepted this as normal at that time of my life, and really never gave the situation a second thought. At our house, one day, my mother asked me to go down town and bring back a loaf of bread. I say down town because we lived on the side of a steep hill which had a slope of around forty five degrees to the horizontal. Five minutes later my mother came back into the living room and asked me why I had not done what she had asked of me. I told her that the bread was on the kitchen table to which she responded that I could not possible have done the errand and be back already. Never-the-less, the loaf of bread was there, in all its glory, for all to see.

As I got older, and grew some more, I was invariably running up hill and down dale. Our house was only half way up the hillside and above us was a wonderful place where I spent a considerable part of my early life.We called it the Barley and after

34

I passed Bushy Park there was only a scattering of cottages and farm houses then acres and acres of wide open moorlands. Sometimes in the company of friends, but usually totally on my own, I would explore every nook and cranny. I could go wild up there but when the sun started to sink in the west, I had just enough time to run down to home before it went completely dark. With all that exercise and fresh mountain air, my head would hit the pillow and I would be in a deep sleep in next to no time. Most of the time, as I was exploring, my parents had no idea where I was or what I was doing during those care free days. Apart from self inflicted injuries, such as falling out of a tree, I was safe as houses and on many occasions never encountered any other living souls up there in that wonderland. Of course, all this running up and down hillsides molded me into a wirey tough little athlete, even though I never realized it at the time. From the age of eight I played soccer until I went to Abersychan Tech. where I was introduced to rugby. I excelled at such endurance sports mainly due to my lung capacity and stamina. When many around me began to flag, I still had energy to spare which kept me running right up to the final whistle. After being selected for the school team I was then spotted by a person who encouraged me to take a job at one of the local factories, however, his ultimate goal was to have me play for their renowned rugby team. The only draw back, which I did not realize when I signed on, was that the team didn't play in my home town region. As all the friends that I grew up with played locally, around Pontypool, all my games were away in the Newport District League. Our team was, in fact, a select team with boys from Blaenavon down to Newport and from Abergavenny over to Newbridge and Abertillery. On two consecutive years this team won the Newport Junior Cup and not a single player was over the age of twenty one. In my particular case I was just sixteen and seventeen during that exciting period. Half of these young men went on to play rugby with some of the best senior teams in Wales. I did the same but with a club up in Cheshire, England. I had moved there to better my job prospect which, as it so happens, worked out amazingly well. On quite a few occasions, during my rugby playing days, I have caught the ball and run the whole length of the field to score. This is more impressive when it is considered that, unlike American football, no blocking or impeding of a rival tackler is allowed and so I had to elude them entirely by myself.

It was during this time, of being an apprentice while working at Girlig Ltd, that I was introduced to road running. Each morning we apprentices had a one hour physical education period which began with exercise then finished off with a five mile run around the local roads. Up until this point I had only run alone and so I had no indication of how good I actually was. Now for the first time, running along side twenty or so other lads, of around my own age, I became keenly competitive and put all my energy into winning these runs. Being one of the youngest and smallest of the bunch I found that I could pull away from the rest of my peers with impunity. I would run along with the others but with a mile to go I would simply increase my pace and end up back at the company field long before the others would arrive. For the next three years, until I left the area, I was selected for the company's athletic team which meant competitive races at field track and road races and I swept the board in all events. It was while I was competing in the Welsh Boys Championships, at Pontypridd, that I found out why I was able to run so effortlessly. I had just finished the three mile event, as a total unknown, and I won by beating some highly favored athletes who had represented Wales. After the race I was surrounded by reporters questioning who I was and where had I suddenly come from. Then I was approached by a famous athletic coaches, of that time, who asked me if he could check my heart. He took out a stethascope and pressed it against my chest and after a few minutes he said "Just as I thought, you have an athlete's heart." After a grueling three mile race my heart was just beating at the pace of a person who had just taken a brisk walk. He was astounded when he found out that I had never belonged

36

to a major athletic club and I had never been formally coached. He asked if I would liked to be introduced to one such club but I was happy just being a renegade runner from the valleys.

I finished competitive running at around the age of twenty eight but I carried on playing rugby until I was thirty six and only finished then because I moved on to America. I scored the winning try [touch down] at the last game that I played in and at the same time I managed to dislocate my right shoulder. Three months after arriving in the Detroit, Michigan area, I was asked to play soccer for a team of ex Brits who played out of an Irish bar. This launched me back into active competition which provided yet another successful and eventful sporting career. I played with this same bunch of guys in the Detroit League, the Great Lakes League and finally the Michigan United League. I played for the Dearborn Rovers for most of this time but finished up with Ferndale Internationals and finally the Canton Celtics. I played my last soccer game in Michigan at the age of fifty nine when I then moved on to Florida. For two years, after arriving in Florida, I played Sunday kick around soccer with a group of mainly Mexican players but at the age of sixty two I decided to retire. Now you would think that this was probably a wise thing to do, at that tender age, but at sixty seven I was coaxed into brushing the cob webs off my boots and to re-enter the fray once more. I did this with a great bunch of guys, who are my new best friends, to this day. In spite of all the bumps, bruises, aches and pains I have never regretted it for one moment and it has given me a new lease of life. After around three years, of this, we were approached to enter a new open aged league to be formed on Anna Maria Island. Bearing in mind that I was now seventy, I would now be playing against players as young as eighteen and up. Our gang agreed to join and have been engaged in this league for the passed five years. So this now brings me up to the age of seventy five and I am still running with this 'ole heart of mine still pumping away. We play Spring and Fall and three sessions ago my team won the Championship Cup which probable puts me as the oldest soccer player in the world. Some people have encouraged me to contact the Guiness Book of Records to make this official because the current holder is a Mexican man who played until he was seventy three. My modesty has prevented me from doing so and, quite honestly, nothing could be more satisfying than the friendships that I have formed throughout the years in all my various sports.

Both my father's and my mother's side, of our family, have lived to fine old ages with their life spans being between the mid eighties to mid nineties. This being the norm, for the Clarke and the Herbert families, I am quite confidant that my heart, barring accidents, should see me well into that age range. I know that my family genes have a great deal to do with my fortunate state of health but I would like to say that looking after what God has given me is also important. For instance, I have never smoke cigarettes in my entire life and when it comes to alcohol , in the main, I only drink light beer. As a puny kid my mother always insisted that I drank lots of milk which she maintained would produce strong bones, and this I still do to this very day. With these simple yet positive health benefits, all put together, I have built a great life and I still, to this very day, feel full of energy. However, having said all this, it is this 'ole heart of mine that allows me to be athletic and healthy, in difference to ninety five percent of the world's population. My strong heart has been the bed rock of all that I have been able to achieve in all the sporting activities that I have participated in throughout my entire life. I could not have wished for a more profound gift to assist and nurture me through lifes rigorous trials and tribulations. There is one other important thing that I must mention and this is that since my heart functions so efficiently, my apperance is of a man who looks ten years younger than my biological age. This has been a considerable boon for me, during my vicarious life, and has rewarded me with many pleasurable experiences which otherwise would not have come my way. For instance my first English wife was five years younger than me and my second and third American wives are fifteen years younger. When I was playing rugby at Port Sunlight, at the age of thirty six, with my youthful appearance I was jokingly dubbed the oldest teenager in the club. All the various facets of this slow beating 'ole heart of mine has made me undeniably fortunate and blissfully happy. To be the innocent recipient of such an almost unbelievable natural gift, is nothing short of a modern day miracle. I guess good fortune is, after all, better than good luck.

CHAPTER SIX

A Shadow In The Sun

I have lived on the paradise island of Anna Maria, Florida for the past sixteen years or so and, in the main, my stay here has been nothing short of idyllic. The beautiful weather, the flora and fauna, the smiling faces and the care free life style all have afforded me an exceptional existence. This blissful little island, with all its beauties, has soothed my savage brow and given me a much brighter life in spite of the rest of the world's stressful and disturbing events. While the rest of the human race seems to be bogged down, with the miseries and woes of life's negativity, this little piece of heaven on earth has maintained the status quo for excellent living. I have never, in my checkered career, been so happy and contented and I am convinced that this care free life style will add extra years to my life expectancy. However, there has been one sorrowful episode which has cast a shadow on this island's otherwise wonderful record of peace and tranquility.

Seven years ago a vivacious, prominent island business woman suddenly and mysteriously disappeared. This particular woman was the co-owner, with her estranged husband, of one of the island's better known quaint little hotels. Her disappearance was a shock, to just about everyone who knew her, and immediately sparked a massive search. Although she and her husband, had a congenial relationship they lived separately. During this time she met a younger man, who was an ex jailbird, and eventually he moved into her rented house up in Anna Maria town. The police interviewed him extensively but he claimed that he had absolutely no idea as to her where about. Several days after she went missing her car was spotted being driven by a Latino man who was immediately pulled in for questioning. He maintained that he had noticed the car, late one night, parked outside of the Gator Lounge on 14th Street, in Bradenton. The bar was closing and he saw that the keys were left in the ignition and the opportunity was too tempting for him to resist. This made him an immediate suspect in connection to the disappearance of the island business lady in question. In parallel with this the police were still interviewing the husband and the live-in boy friend as to their whereabouts and movements and checked their alibis for the night that she was last seen. Rumors swirled as half of the island residents thought that the husband was possibly guilty, of some foul deed, while the other half thought the same about the boy friend. No matter where you went, on the island, it was rife with suspicions and speculation concerning this untypical island mystery. As it so happened about six weeks, before all this, my wife and I were invited to a house party, in Palmetto, held by another couple of married island hoteliers. We were seated on the same table with this very lady and her husband and we enjoyed plenty of good conversation and humor with them for several hours until they left around midnight.

Then less than a week before she disappeared my wife took her two grand daughters to their hotel to see the Halloween decorations that they had on display. A load of various candies were laid on for the children to take, for their treats, and lots of scary stuff to amuse everyone. My wife saw her there but, as you can imagine, with the hotel being full of children running around with great excitement it made conversation difficult. Apart from a casual acknowledgement she just smiled and thanked our family group for attending her special event. She was known for her kindness and worked at any events run by local business owners for the benefit of the island residents. She was considered, by all, who met her, as a breath of fresh air and was almost always full of enthusiasm. Her husband, on the other hand, was a less public figure who kept himself to himself and doggedly concentrated on the running of their hotel business. Around that particular time on the weekends, because they still had a fairly amiable relationship, they could sometimes be seen having dinner at one, or other, of our many local restaurants. As far as I can recall, I never saw her in public with her boy friend and I suspect that he might not have had the same level of intellect that she had acquired on being brought up and schooled in Germany. However, I must point out that this is merely conjecture, on my part, and is simply derived from unverified snippets of information which I have heard concerning their different back grounds.

During the police investigation it was found out that the boy friend had broken his probation, on a previous arson charge , and so he was immediately sent back to prison for thirteen years. He steadfastly stuck to his story that he had no idea what had happened to her that night and said that they had an argument, over some trivial incident, and she had stormed out of the house without saying where she was going. Of course, they were also questioning her husband at length but he said that he had not seen her, on the night in question, and therefore could not help them with their inquiries. A third possibility came into the equation when it was reported that she had been seen at Tampa International Airport boarding a plane for Europe. Our island was buzzing with rumors and innuendos as everyone put forward their ideas as to which of the two principle characters was the guilty party. Then, as the whole incident was slightly waning there came an event that stoked the fire from smoldering back to aflame again. About a year after this lady went missing a suit case was found, on garbage day, out in front of the hotel. This was given to the police and when they opened it, there was many of this lady's personal affects. The husband casually said that he could not bear to deal with them, at the hotel anymore, since it was fairly obvious that after all this time it was unlikely that she would return. During the following years, on a few occasions, some lady's personal items would found on the beach, at various locations, which sparked the police to bring out the cadaver dogs. Then bulldozers would be brought in and those particular areas, of our beaches, would be plowed up and several days were spent with the police scrupulously delving in the sand. However, all this diligent work came to no avail.

After around five years the police decided that they had enough evidence to charge the boy friend with her murder, even though a body had not been found. In spite of all the years of questioning the boy friend stubbornly refused to give up any information about the actual murder or where her body could be found. For the next two years the boy friends defense attorneys dragged out the court proceedings for as long as they possibly could. They proceeded to file several continuances, one after another, in the hope that time would dim this tragic event in their client's favor. Seven years had now gone by and finally the boy friend had his day in court and stood in front of a judge. To the total shock of everyone involved he pleaded guilty to second degree murder because, in his theory, it was not premeditated. He said that it all started, innocuously, with an argument about him smoking indoors and with his record, of setting a previous girl friends house on fire, this was completely understandable. Apparently the argument then escalated to a level where she stated that she could not carry on with their fractured relationship anymore. At this point he punched her and then, in a fit of rage, strangled her until she was lifeless. He then wrapped her, in a bed sheet, and cautiously put her into the back seat of her car. He then drove over to the hotel to get a shovel and, having been a part time handyman there, he knew exactly where it was stored. Then he drove to 81st Street, Holmes Beach, just around the corner from the hotel, where he parked and removed her from the car. He then carried her to the beach where he buried her four foot down. He then cleverly discarded her purse, at a different location, just to confuse anyone looking for her. The next day he drove her car to the Gator Lounge, leaving the keys where they could be easily be seen. Then he calmly caught the public transport bus back to the island where he then rode the trolley back to her house on Magnolia Avenue. This confession was in return for him having two years off his twenty two year murder sentence. Finally everyone knew what took place and subsequently what had happened to her on that fateful night of November the 4th, 2008. A huge combined sigh of relief could now be heard all over our island.

There still remained just one question to be answered and that was concerning the exact location of where her body was buried. Just about everyone, on this island, knew that the most probable site had to be somewhere on the beach near 81st Street but that still left thousands of places to be investigated. On Friday the 23rd of October, almost exactly seven years to the day that she went missing, the police brought her ex boy friend to this island. On the beach, without hesitation, he calmly walked directly to a spot and identified it as being where he had buried her. He didn't have to stop and look around the dunes or the beach because this spot was significant and had not altered over the duration of this case. She was buried under a four posted public cabana, about twelve foot square, which had been put there for beach goers to use as a shelter, from the sun, and as a picnic convenience. The police were confounded when shown the burial location because for the passed seven years families had been using this very spot to enjoy themselves in a party atmosphere. Unbeknown to them the missing woman lay just four feet under the sand of the area which they were using for their joyous occasions. The police asked him, with all the miles of beaches that he could have used, why did he choose this location. He quite simply said that he thought it would be the most unlikely place for any searchers to suspect as a burial sight. He deliberately chose this site because, in his mind, the police would automatically search the other more remote and unpopular spots. This is exactly what they did, for seven long years, while he kept this information, as an ace up his devious sleeve, to be pawned when the right time came. If I have learned anything in life it is that a person doesn't need to go to a university and get a degree in street smart. Years of dishonesty and conniving, to outsmart the police, is the only edges a criminal needs to keep just one step ahead of the law. Never the less, as in this unfortunate episode, the law usually wins in the end. I have found that there is nothing more thought provoking than the confinement of a prison cell to make felons repent the devious deeds that they have perpetrated during their wretched lives. In the end the felon's guilt will weigh so heavily that they inevitably have to divulge their wrongful deeds. It could be said that the sands of time ran out for this wretched human being.

Everyone involved finally had the closure they so deserve concerning this painful event. The husband, God bless his soul, is out from under the veil of suspicion and can hopefully pick up the pieces of his shattered life. For purely business reasons he had an insurance policy, on his estranged wife, which he was not allowed to claim until her demise was positively brought to light and he was cleared of all wrong doings. Her son and grand children can now relax but I am sure that their days out at the beach will never again involve that sinister beach pavilion. All her long time island friends had a proper memorial service for her where they talked about the times when she was alive and vibrant. Anna Maria Island can hopefully carry on in it's usual care free manner without this dark shadow looming over their shoulder. This whole affair was somewhat surreal to me as I had never before, in my life, personally known someone who was violently murdered. You can read about this kind of thing almost every day in the news papers or hear of them on the television but when the fatality is some-one that you have known, this is a whole different scenario. Now that the killer has come clean, and offered the victim's family and friends the chance to heal, peace and serenity has finally returned to this wonderful island. Each evening, as we witness the going down of the sun, we can think of her and she will be remembered as a bright and beautiful ray of sunshine. For many people here she will be sorely missed. Incidentally, this whole riveting story has just recently been shown on the television's nationally syndicated program "Dateline."

To sum up, as far as humanity is concerned there are certain social lines that we as human beings are forbidden, and thus expected, not to cross. Such perpetrators, of these murderous crimes, should be considered as the carbuncles on the arse of society. Since we never know when it is our time to go, we can only hope that it will be in a dignified manner and not in a fit of jealous rage. When a life is taken in a violent way the guilty party will always, somewhere down the line, have to pay the piper. We can only hope that when it is our time to depart, this bountiful world, that it will be predictably calm and civilized. I say this because I feel that to die, at the hands of a murderer, in a savage and misguided event, somewhat detracts from all the good things that we have worked for and garnered during a wonderful and productive span of life. For anyone to finish their existence, in such a sordid manner, it would be a devastating anti-climax and thus over shadow all previous positive and meaningful achievements. Amen.

CHAPTER SEVEN

Viva la Difference

I have lived half of my life in Britain and the other half in America, more aptly, the United States. Because of this fact, when engaged in conversation, I am quite often asked questions concerning the cultural differences between the two nations. Since American's have European, African, Asian, Native Indian and many other nation's blood , running through their veins, one might assume that there would be more differences than similarities. Because of the relatively short time period, of the New World being discovered, America has had a lot of catching up to do. In it's headlong rush to match the other civilized parts of the world, America has come a long way in a relatively short period of time. Quite often many swift actions and decisions, concerning various problems, actually preceding the law of the land. In the conception only the east coast region, of the newly found America, was civilized and in any way conformed to European justice. As settlers spread west, away from the major eastern coast cities such as New York, Boston, Baltimore, Philadelphia and Washington, in many places there was no civilized law at all. The original New England States were formed before, and sometimes during, the war between the British and the French colonists of that region which bordered on to-day's Canada. To say nothing of the ongoing Indian Wars, with various tribes, which were continually breaking out at any given time. Once the French War finished, defining the border between America and Canada, the newly shaped nation could now begin to look inward and establish an acceptable code of conduct. Still, at this point, under the distant yoke of the British government, and all the taxations that were imposed upon them, the American settlers began resenting this affront to their existence. Then another war ensued to rid the interference in their daily lives, by the British government, which became a ten year drawn out war for complete independence.

For many years, after the first colonizing of these lands, individual trappers and mountain men set out to discover new horizons. Later, large groups of settlers headed west in their search of spacious skies and infinite freedom. They push onward not knowing how vast the land was, where they were going, what it would take to get there or even where they would eventually end up. The severity of these journeys were, in many cases, over whelming and many of these brave but naïve people died trying to achieve their lifetime dreams of independence. There is a new movie, which has just been released, entitle "A Million Ways to Die in the West" and although it's contents was a spoof, it could not be more true. The term "run for your life" came about when if captured, by some forest Indian tribes, they would give you about one hundred yards start. Then the whole war party would come running after you with spears, tomahawks and knives and would hack you to death if they caught up to you. Literally thousands of the early settlers, men, women and children, met their doom when traveling through Indian territories. Not only native Indians were to be feared but also snakes, bears, cougars and other deadly animals which took their toll on these intrepid travelers. Then there was the terrain with many wide, deep fast flowing rivers, precipitous mountainous trails and scorching hot arid deserts to be contended with. Added to all this was nature's wrath which brought forth fierce thunder and lightning storms, torrential rains and even vast prairie fires. Remember these travelers had no permanent housing, just covered wagons and tents to live in. It is quite remarkable that any of these gritty people survived at all but they did and that is how America was born one place at a time. From these places came towns and from some towns came cities and from these cities came a new country and a nation of diverse people. Then the introduction of the railways joined many major large centers of population as the nation expanded.

After the opening of the regions, west of the Mississippi River, there was yet another traumatic period in the on going saga of the American nation. This was the Civil War, between the Northern and Southern States which pitted and divided family members against each other. Hundreds of thousands of men and boys were killed during this four year period and it took many latter years to rebuild this shattered country. This meant that in a period, of roughly two hundred years, the citizens of this fledgling nation had to endure three major, and I do mean major, wars. Now I am aware of the fact that many Europeans have seen a goodly amount, of these fascinating stories, depicted in Hollywood western and war movies but it is one thing to watch a re-enactment but it is a completely different case to actually have lived through such hard grueling events. My highlighting of these historic times is to enlighten people to the fact that these many deadly and horrific events, in America, up until a little over a hundred and fifty years ago. All this has led to the molding of a tough, uncompromising and gritty nation of people who have lived and survived through untold hardships and adversity. These people have learned how a poorly timed or bad decision could adversely affect the outcome of their entire lives. I mean if you are standing out in the street in Dodge City, facing another gun man, and he shouts "Draw" you have a second or two to make a decision. This is a life or death situation and you had better not hesitate as the outcome will certainly not be going in your favor. In the best scenario you will most definitely be wounded and in the worse situation you will be dead.

The fact that with the influx of so many different nationalities, within this confined country, this has engendered fierce internal competition on just about every social level. This immigrant country, with its various mixed nationalities eager and willing to get ahead of each other has generated such rivalry, on many levels, which overtook politeness and political correctness. While other peoples, with their own particular inbred foibles might hesitate, in general an American's unrestricted outlook on life enabled him to make an immediate decision without hesitating. While other nationalities will debate a subject at length an American, with the mantra that action speaks louder than words, will strike while the iron is hot. To others, on some occasions, this might seem rude or crass but it is easier to fix a fast decision than make a bad one or not make one at all. A good example of this was in World War II, when Eisenhower was Commander of the entire Allied Army , he had quite a few disagreements with Montgomery, the British General, as their upbringings meant that they could not see eye to eye on numerous situations. Monty preferred the cautious approach whereas Ike was accustomed to the ploy of direct action. Their outlook on the same problem was usually opposites and I am not saying that either of them was always right or always wrong, it was just their different ways of looking at the same problem. When bold and decisive decisions had to be made quickly Eisenhower's skill, in that department, came through loud and clear. This , I believe, was a distinct and undisputable result from each of their different up bringing. Luckily for us all, on the allied side, they worked around their differences of opinion and got that immense job done with a strained yet workable harmony.

Almost every morning, here on Anna Maria Island, I go for coffee on the beach across the road from my house. I observe family parties coming in bringing young children with them. It is, to me, interesting to watch the differing dynamics between American families compared with European families. On approaching their designated table the American family will, almost always, ask their nubile off springs where they would like to sit. The child being too young and inexperienced to make a decision is stymied and then a protracted conference invariably ensues. When a European family approaches their table there is no fuss because the children are told where to sit and everything goes off like clockwork. I merely mention this as an example of the different ways of parenting and the outcome that this brings. After the American children grow up, because of their early freedom of choice, they become much more independent and much more likely to take chances at an younger age. Due to this, like Eisenhower, they are less inhibited and more apt to take a calculated risks. On the other hand the European children grow up in a more predictable environment and will lead a more structured life. This results in not too many major failures or successes but a well balanced life where it is easier to fit in because virtually everyone is on the same page. It is a simple case of conformity, in the one case, verses individualism in the other. Americans are more likely to succeed at individual events and the Europeans are better at working on group projects together. For example America has had many individual athletes , who seem to come out of nowhere, spread across many sports where lone fortitude seems the key to their success. Europeans seem to have better results at team sports, in international contests, and two that immediately spring to mind is their Ryder Cup golf team and the German national soccer team that has won the soccer World Cup four times. I want to be quite clear that I am not, in any way, suggesting that either one is better than the other. I am just trying to explain my views of the differences on both sides of the coin.

When talking to European visitors there are three inevitable questions that almost always arise when considering life in America compared to their homelands. I am only going to elude to them briefly as all three of these are deep and complicated and warrant a entire book, of their own, dedicated to each subject. The first is the question of gun control and how the possession of fire arms affects the general public and the conditions of living in America. To begin with I must say that the right to bear arms is deeply rooted in Amendment II of the America's Constitution since just after the War of Independence from Britain. That war was basically won because all the settlers had guns, for their family's protection, and were able to form quickly assembled militias to fight the Red Coats. Since then guns have been used to ward off savage wild animals, violent criminals and, more recently, extreme terrorists. It is echoed, throughout the USA, that if guns were banned, only the criminals would have them. The gun enthusiasts here also say "I will give up my gun when it is pried from my cold, dead hand." In other words never. I have never owned a gun or ever fired one but there have been a few uncomfortable occasions when I would have felt more secure if I had one. Yes there has been other times, throughout this country's history, when things have gone horribly wrong and the results have been unnecessary deaths. However, when on extreme occasions, your family or possessions are being threatened, a gun could come in handy and even save the day. It is a fifty/fifty split vote and so long as the National Rifle Association exists it will remain contentious for many years to come, if not forever.

The second subject for debate is always Health Care and all it's complicated ramifications. In most European nations they have socialized medical care which basically means that taxes are taken out of a persons earnings and put aside to be used at a later date when needed. The tax rate in these countries is proportionately higher to accommodate this system which means that it is then free at the time of want because it has been previously paid for. In America each individual is taxed less but with that extra money earn they, themselves, must take out and pay for insurance to cover any later required treatments. If poor people cannot afford insurance there are built in systems available from the government, to handle these but it can be long, confusing and frustrating. Of course if you have money anything is possible and some famous and wealthy Europeans, particularly professional athletes, come to the USA to get specialized treatments. The medical industry is, in many cases, more modern and far superior herein America and it shocks me to see the general condition of hospitals in Britain. I personally have known friends, over there, who have died while waiting for a bed to become available for them to receive treatment. My own mother was too fragile to live on her own and because of the shortage of available care housings, she was put into a mental ward for the last three months of her life. She was finally moveto a care home but died two weeks later and that was no way for a proud woman to end her days. To sum up there is no such thing as a free lunch when it comes to Health Care, no matter where you live or which system is engaged.

The third subject is that of education and the comparisons between the American and European systems. Having been educated in Britain and have seen the differences here, I feel that I am a good barometer for a discussion of the two systems. Let me say, unquivitably, that the education children receive, across the pond is without a doubt superior to that received by students in America. The basic "Three R's, Reading, Writing and Arithmatic", are taken very seriously and this engenders a consistently good level of education. Other subjects which is considered important for learning are History and Geography which enables the students to be more worldly.Of course the history of Britain is learned from as far back as two thousand years ago whereas American history spans only around four to five hundred years back. With my geographical knowledge I have found that students in Britain, and probably Europe, are far more in tune with world wide affairs. Where as quite often, in America, young people don't know the capitol cities of their surrounding States, let alone the capitols of their surrounding countries. So, in a nut shell, the average non American student is much better prepared with knowledge of the world in general.

Now we have to ask the question as to whether this gives the British students a better chance, of favorably progress in life, when they finish their education and leave school? For the average teenager, across the pond, the answer is not necessarily so. This is because I personally have known young people who have come out of college with degrees to find out that there are no jobs available in their chosen careers. They have sometimes been wrongly directed in a manner that leads them down a blind alley. Not every child is college material and so instead of forcing them, in the wrong direction, it is better to assess their abilities before insisting on a flight of fancy that leads to a dead end. In the western world, we need people in the skilled trades department such as auto- mechanics, plumbers, carpenters, stone masons and electricians. At the age of sixteen, two years before they graduate, youngsters should be trained in a vocational school which should be considered as the first two years of their degree. After graduating from this school they should then be given two more years in college to achieve a degree in his/her chosen trade. This makes much more sense than coming out with some obscure degree which cannot be easily used and now having high education loans to pay. From the age of sixteen I trained for five year as an engineering apprenticeship at a manufacturing company which meant I was trained and became a fully qualified engineer at twenty one years of age which jump started my career. Education should return to this format.

Turning to the American scene, much of what I have just expounded also applies here. Although, as I have previously stated, the standard of education is not so high, in specific subjects, America has a lot to offer in different areas. So far as almost any sport and music training is concerned the USA is head and shoulders above almost any other country in the world. In the music arena students can learn to play an instrument and join the schools marching band. They can also sing in a choir and even put on musical stage shows. Students can indulge themselves in football, baseball, soccer, swimming, golf, volleyball or track and cross country running. Each high school, in any given county, is highly competitively motivated and wants to be the champions of their particular sporting activity. College and University scouts continually watch these athletes and, if they are good enough, a fully paid scholarships can be awarded to gifted athletes. This opens up a whole slew of opportunities that are, in Europe, generally only offered to a select few. To get in on this wave of success, in these arenas, young people from outside of the USA, with high skill levels, are coming to America to try and make their dreams come true. Once again, as pointed out before, the education systems of the two global areas are different but in the final analysis neither one is better than the other. As depicted, in a time worn adage, it is simply a case of horses for courses.

CHAPTER EIGHT
A Bitter Pill To Swallow

Political correctness is, without a doubt, the biggest load of tripe, inflicted upon us as a direct result of a code devised by a sector of Utopian minded attorneys who will take any law case, no matter how trivial, to benefit themselves. Don't get me wrong, there are some blatant words and actions that should be struck from the annuls of mankind but now, alas, it has gone way too far. For instance, I recently used the term "gypsy" and was told that saying this word was no longer socially acceptable. Ever since Biblical times this was a regularly used description of a class for people but somewhere, somehow, someone has decided this term can no longer be used. Apparently the powers that be have decided to rename this mainly dishonest group of people as Travelers. Here, in America, they can still go freely from State to State ripping off elderly folk, of their hard earned monies, with their bogus drive way repairing and re-roofing scams but their feelings might be sorely offended if they are referred to as gypsy. At another instance I innocently said that "I call a spade, a spade" meaning that I don't mince words. Here again I was informed that such sayings are no longer acceptable in this sensitive age that we now live in. I guess that referring to a Cadillac as a "Jewish canoe" is now also taboo. Because the USA is a melting pot of many nationalities it appears that the minorities, particular the more recent immigrants, are given preference over the majority which to me seems to be wrong. In France there is now a law prohibiting Islamic women from wearing the burqa in public because men terrorist can dress in them to commit acts of mayhem. This makes perfect sense because it protects the majority of citizens against criminal acts by minority sects. Yet in America our attorneys insist that this could be consider unconstitutional.

In the years gone by all immigrants, to the USA, had to work hard to be accepted into our society but now, it appears, that we allow new immigrants immediate equal rights even though they have done nothing to warrant it. When this happens it is frowned upon if any long established nationals complain or show any form of resentment against this absurd set of circumstances. It is getting so mundane that Christians cannot pray in public and patriots cannot show the American flag for fear of offending a person of a different culture. High school and college students are forbidden from wearing tee-shirts or caps with the Stars and Stripes on them incase, in the remote possibility, this action should cause the more recent immigrants to be upset. Even Halloween costumes are now under scrutiny where consultants can advise you as to whether or not your innocent choice of dressing up is likely to be offensive. Is there no end to this ludicrous state of affairs! In many such cases ours own laws, which were installed hundreds of years ago, are now used against us. To gain an advantage an immigrant, who has been given the hospitality of entering our country, immediately wants to change things to suit his/her past traditions brought with them from a foreign land. All this has predictably engendered a landslide of frivolous law suits which is really what the attorneys, who I previously mentioned, had hoped for. This is what political correctness, the thin end of the wedge to socialism, can eventually bring if we accept the changes that a small liberal sector wants us to obey. It is a fact of life that there will always be the "haves" and "have-nots" in society but forcing political correctness down everyone's throat, in an attempt to make us all equal, is a misguided and unattainable practice. Having everyone at the same social level has been tried before, it is called Communism. If the minority, of so called do-gooders, want this lifestyle they should relocate to North Korea and endure a totally predictable and regulated life style. In that controlled environment they can experience what having their thoughts and actions predetermined for them is really like.

There is one glimmer of hope, on the horizon, and it comes from a very unlikely and totally unexpected source. The political scene is ramping up for the upcoming 2016 Presidential election and the charismatic Donald Trump, a breath of fresh air, has entered the race. I don't know what would happen if he was elected, as our next President, but he has certainly stirred up the waters. Because of his vast wealth he is not afraid to tell it as it is and is not daunted by any attorney threats. They will not take him on, for his political incorrectness, because his pockets are so deep they are concerned that he will put them out of business if they even think of suing him. This basically proves, what I have been saying all along, that some attorneys have concocted this fiasco to line their own pockets. He does not abide by main stream politics and even vilifies the press for their one sided and often misguided view points. On a recent televised Republican party Presidential Candidate debate, Trump took the moderators to task for asking improper, unfounded and inaccurate questions during this important national forum. He is so used to being in a top level business mode that, without having to weigh his words, he is forth right and says exactly what he is thinking. In these days, of mealy mouthed and puny politicians, this is indeed a much needed shot in the arm. Other lesser politicians evade from directly answering these types of delicate questions. If they do answer, they tiptoe around it for fear that their real opinions will trip them up and render them as being politically incorrect. It is quite often embarrassing to watch their antics as they stumble around, avoiding their true views , to come up with an answer that they feel will render them politically correct. Harry Truman, one of our past leading Presidents, is famous for saying "The buck stops here" but most of our present day politicians are more unfavorably inclined to pass the buck.

As I have previously said, I don't think Trump can make a good President because he is not diplomatically savvy. However, through his top level business deals, he has developed into a hard hitting, no nonsense negotiator and is not likely to give the farm away to foreign interests. He is completely at ease when it comes down to getting his own way so if he can do this for America, as a nation, this will without a doubt be to our distinct advantage. I mean swapping one army deserter for five top Al Qaeda terrorist was just about the most inane political decision that I have encountered in my protracted life time. I am not for one political party or another, it is simply a matter of common sense because several of these released terrorists are back fighting against us again. We need a leader who will say that deals, such as this, are completely out of the question and should not have ever been considered in the first place. If Donald Trump was involved I am sure these negotiations would have gone in our favor. Trump's outlandish manner of speaking can be toned down, by his advisors, but his brand of direct confrontation cannot be instilled into other less brave politicians who are paralyzed by this political correctness. I can assure you that I do not intend for this to be a party political rant but I just want to make it known that, in these uncertain times, America needs a firm and resilient leader. The Russian leader Putin marched into the Crimea because his country needed a port on the Black Sea. He is the most politically incorrect person, probably in the world, but in his home land he is idolized as a hero and doesn't give a care what the rest of the world thinks of him. The introduction of political correctness has made us a weaker nation in the eyes of our enemies. They understand that this blight, on our society, has sapped the impetus from our decision maker's thought process and replaced it with doubt and uncertainty. When we had the chance to kill Bin Laden our legal advisors said that we could not do so because he was attending a funeral and it took another ten years before the chance presented itself again. Not only was he let off the hook but just about every prominent Al Quida leader was present and this strike would have wiped out their whole chain of command in one stroke. Thanks to political correctness we are a weaker nation.

CHAPTER NINE
The Crème de la Crème

It is a well known fact that I am an avid Rugby fan. Having played this rugged sport for twenty five years, from the age of ten, the love for this game runs through my veins and is deeply ensconced in my heart. The climax of this sport is a tournament where all the rugby playing countries, from around the globe, come together to decide who is the champion nation of the world. Unlike America's baseball, so called, World Series this is a multi-national event which is fiercely competed for at the highest level of fitness and toughness. The winner of this competition holds the title for four years, just like the world soccer champions, which means that this country rules the roost, with all its attached glories, until another team knocks them off their perch. The most recent of these events, hosted at England and Wales, has just ended with the champions being the great New Zealand team, has just concluded. Was it not for the fact that I flew over to Wales for a family wedding, three months before this event, I would have been present for this prestigious tournament but , alas, I was not able to return there within such a short time span. I had to be satisfied with watching the whole event on my television, from America, instead of soaking up the atmosphere of being there in person. I missed the rabid fans, all decked out in their county's colors, the camaraderie of the different nationalities and the meeting of long lost friends from around the world. Yes, the games are brutal but a person has to experience this event to truly know the meaning of deep and lasting friendships. As hard and frantic as it gets, on the field, when the game is over everyone shakes hands and enjoy a beer with each other. It is a pity that other sports do not follow rugby's tradition of players and fans shaking hands, after the game, to show no hard feelings. I feel this act is better than other traditions of shaking of hands before the game.

I had to restrict my viewing of these amazing games, from here in America, because Pay Per View were charging $32 per game however, I was able to watch the two semi-finals and the final. My beloved Welsh team were defeated, in virtually the last minute of their game, at the quarter final stage, by South Africa with a score of 26 points to 23. In the semis New Zealand beat South Africa and Australia beat Argentina to produce a final where the number one and the number two rated teams in the world would face off against each other. This would turn out to be a colossal battle between some of the mightiest men, from around the world, with no quarters being given and none being asked. As this top match of the world kicked off I saw a familiar face, on the pitch, and I realized that I had met this person not more than three months earlier. This was, no less than, rugby world's number one referee the irrepressible Nigel Owens. On my recent visit back, to my home town of Pontypool, I was invited on a trip to Brynmawr Rugby Club where the guest speaker was to be the very same man. It was inspiring to hear Nigel talk and some of his stories, concerning humorous episodes, while refereeing games, were highly entertaining. At this particular time the appointments of referees, for the World Cup, had not been announced and so no-one present, that Sunday afternoon, had any idea that the man they were listening to would be given the most important game in the rugby world. It was refreshing to hear his views concerning rugby and afterwards he answered questions, from the audience, on the finer points of the game. Before he left I lined up to get his autograph which now resides in my book along with many other famous sports celebrities. I chatted to him briefly and he told me that he was pleased that the game of rugby was now taking hold in America. I shook his hand and wished him well and I would like to think that it was this that rocketed him to his now famous status as being the number one in the world. Incidentally, Brynmawr Rugby Club must be congratulated for hosting this well organized event as everything went off like clockwork. Their youth team players did an excellent job of bussing the tables. It is sad though, for me, to see that they have a better club house than my home town where they now use a small local pub as their head quarters. For my Welsh friends I want to inform them that there is an area, just outside Philadelphia, Pennsylvania called Brynmawr.

It has been my good fortune, throughout my wandering life, to have met some of the most influential people in the sporting and music sector of entertainment. In every case I have found these people to be humble and sincere that is so long as you know how to behave in their presence. In your time with them if you treat them like normal people, which they basically are, they will treat you as an equal. On the other hand if you go gaga their reaction will be to want to be rid of you as quickly as possible. At the local Moose Lodge, here on Anna Maria Island, over a period of time I happen to be involved in several casual conversation with a new member. It was just friendly and not too serious banter so we never did talk about who we were or what we did. As a matter of fact we didn't even know each others names and he mistakenly referred to me as Irish. About two months, into this casual relationship, I come to find out just who this friendly new Moose member was. It turned out that this modest man's name was Johnny Lattner who had been a famous American Football player and also a coach in his latter playing days. So now I knew who he was but because his hey days was way before I came to the USA, I had to look up the details of his playing career. He played half back for the Notre Dame University out of South Bend, Indiana or the Fighting Irish as they are more popularly known. He was a prolific scorer and during his time in that team, they only lost three times during three years. He was awarded the most treasured trophy, in college football, I am referring to the Heisman Memorial Trophy. This means that during his time he was selected at being the best, at what he did, out of all the athletes that were playing football throughout America. He moved on into the professional ranks with the Pittsburgh Steelers but this was interrupted by service in the US Air Force. When he came out of the service he coached for around ten years before opening his, now famous, Steak House in Chicago. The strange thing is that I had previously dined at that very restaurant on several business trips to the Windy City. He told me to drop in and say "Hi" any time I found myself in his neighborhood which, yet again, shows just how serendipitous life can be.

Another example of how normal super stars can be, when they are met, is the 1960's soccer great George Best. He was brought up in a working class district of Belfast, Northern Ireland during what was termed as "the troubled times." This was that disastrous era when secetarian wars were raging between extreme factions of the protestant and catholic religions. At most George was only about five foot six tall and weighed around one hundred and fifty pounds ringing wet. So in these competitive games, he had to be quick of mind and fleet of foot to stay ahead of anyone who might want to stop him. Amazingly, because of his soccer skills, a talent scout for Manchester United spotted him and he was signed on as a member of that prestigious club at fifteen years of age. By the time he was eighteen he had risen to the first team and was competing in England's top division and also in European Cup competitions. Now George was one of the greatest dribblers, of a soccer ball, that had emerged in that sport for many years. He would receive a pass and his only thought was to attack the opposing defence immediately. He was a magician and would mesmerize the other team's players as he mercurially picked his way past them. In todays soccer games attacking players go to ground the minute they are touched but not George. He would try to stay on his feet no matter what happened and I have even seen him keep running a few steps while on this knees. In todays highly proffessional game players are coached to attack the opponents goal by passing the ball out wide to the wings for them to cross it back into the penalty box. However, George ran straight at the goal regardless of where he was on the field or how many defenders were between him and the goal keeper. Sometimes, after beating all the defenders, he would take the ball into the penalty box and then, to everyone's delight, he would dribble around the goalkeeper before putting the ball in the net for yet another amazing goal. He was blessed with audacious skill and endless determination which, during his golden days, made him the European Soccer Player of the year.

It was my pleasure to meet George in the early 1980's when his best playing days were behind him but he was still a charismatic character. He was playing for Fort Lauderdale Strikers against the Detriot Express and I met him at the bar of the Main Event Lounge in Pontiac Silverdome. For around fifteen minutes we were the only two there and I bought us a beer each as we stood there having a casual chat. He was as unassuming as could be with that wry smile and a twinkle in his eye. We talked soccer until Ian Callahan, the ex Liverpool winger, came to get George because the Strikers coach was about to leave for Detroit Metro Airport and catch a plane back to Florida. Our brief time together was spent in a similar manner as two friends who had not seen each other for a while and were catching up on old times. We were both completely at ease but as he was leaving I asked for his autograph because, even back then, I knew that I was in the company of greatness. When I look at todays top soccer players, with their superior fitness and over coaching, they still can't put the ball in the net like George could. As a matter of fact, in today's game he would probably be berated for holding onto the ball too much. Back in the day, his goal was to entertain the crowd which he did whenever he stepped onto the field of play. Off the field, with his notoriety at such a young age, he sadly became a play boy and an avid partier which eventually led him to alcoholism which, in the end, was the cause of his death. Years later I had the good fortune to meet a daughter of his, while on a visit to Murfreesboro, Tennessee and I assured her that he was a kind and caring person and the only one that he ever hurt, in his life time, was himself.

I have been highly fortunate, in my nomadic life, to have been able to travel without constraint and, in doing so, I was lucky enough to meet some of the best known and most charismatic people on this earth. I have been able to meet top personalities from all kinds of competitive sports. American football, soccer, rugby, baseball, ice hockey, golf, motor cycle racing, ballroom dancing and track and field athletics. From the music industry I have met The Beatles, The Who, The Stones, Elton John, Rod Stewart and many other numerous individual artist too many to mention and in every incident the atmosphere was cordial. It should not be forgotten that ,before being thrust into the lime light, all these people were just regular working class stiffs just like us. However, because of some God given talent, or in some cases just pure luck, they have been fortunate enough to step out of the realm of mediocrity and into fame. In Rod's case he was drunk one night, on a London underground train, when an important man in the music industry happened to hear him singing. Long John Baldrey put his business card into his pocket and next morning, not remembering who had done so, Rod phoned him to find out what it was all about and the rest is history. On the other side of the coin a good pal of mine could have been a soccer celebrity if his father had not turned down an offer from a top team who came to his house to sign him to a professional contract. He came home late from school and missed this momentous event and was not told about it until years later after immigrating from England to Canada. Fame can be but a fleeting moment.

CHAPTER TEN
Chaaa~ching

When I first came to Florida I was still employed by a large industrial distribution company out of Livonia, Michigan. I was one of, if not the, leading salesmen working for this outfit but I had already visited the Sunshine State and had made my mind up that, when I retired, this is where I wanted to live. When the company decided that they needed a salesman, in Florida, I immediately marched into the Sales Directors office and, right out, asked for the job. Although I was five years away from retiring I figured I might as well move and settle there ahead of my golden years. The Director gave me the job, right there and then, but warned me that I would not be able to make the same money, down there, that I was now on. At this juncture I had been working happily for this firm for four years but more recently things had changed for the worse. My original company had been bought out and a large ponderous manufacturing conglomerate were now in charge but didn't know the fast paced distribution business. This is not the first time, in my checkered career, that I have been in this position where the new owners have said that their taking over, the original business, would not change the way that they will run the company. However, they just could not resist the urge of making my company operate in the same manner as theirs and this did not work. What a load of bull excrement.

They then bought another small distribution business, which was on the verge of going out of business, then integrating their salesmen into our sales team but paid them more money. All this did not set well with me and, in the back of my mind, moving away was my get out of jail card. My plan was to live there when I retired, at sixty five, so why not go there now ahead of that time and get established. Therefore, the money was not a major issue and did not phase me one bit because, being extremely resourceful, I was sure that somehow I could find a way to make things right. I already knew that quite a few sales representatives, working far away from their home base, were working for more than one company. This could be done quite simply by handing out technical literature, to your existing customer base, and get paid on a direct commission basis. For this purpose I established a dummy company and installed my wife as being the owner. We had a pile of advertising fliers made up, for this new company, with our contact information on and affixed this to all hand out material for our newly acquired list of suppliers. As I traveled around, for my main company, I would also leave this additional information with my contacts and informed them it was for my wife's business. The customers accepted without complaint and so any commissions, made from these deals, were paid to our new company and went into a separate bank account which we had set up for this very purpose. An old saying goes, "There is more than one way to kill a cat than by drowning it." I worked in Florida, for that company, for two more years but they, as I had predicted with their inexperience in this market place, began to fall apart. They now, one by one, began to fire the original company salesmen and I could see the writing on the wall. After two years in Florida they let me go but I had negotiated a nice severance package, which other co-workers did not get, and I am enjoying living off this to this very day. By the time I was let go, at aged sixty two my contingency plan, which I outlined, was now in full swing and my career was set to continue outside of corporate mismanagement.

I worked in this manner for the next two years while I was waiting for my Social Security payments to kick in. I had decided to take Social Security three years earlier than normal but this meant that I would only be getting eighty percent of my full allowance. I also had to wait for my company pension to begin, on the same date, and so I had to look for some other way to make money. I looked at various options but finally decided to buy into the pay phone business which was attractive to me because it was an all cash concern. Because of the nature of this business there was no way that any authority could know exactly how much money I was actually earning. At this time in question cell phones had recently come onto the market and the use of pay phones had dropped quite considerably. It is sad to say that the only people still using pay phones, to any degree, were those unfortunately involved in vicarious enterprises. This type of activity prevails because it is difficult for the police to trace their calls and so drug traffickers, prostitutes, gamblers and illegal aliens made up my customer base. I bought six pay phones at a cost of $3,000 a piece and then had to pay a placement specialist to find me good locations which turned out to be seedy bars and trailer parks. Then I also had to pay an engineer to install them and train me on how to maintain and keep them running. In all it cost me around $24,000 by the time this was all done and dusted. After all this was done, I was left completely on my own to run this precarious business. Once a week I would do the rounds and collect the cash, which was all coins, then wrap them and deposit them at the bank. To be able to do this, with the least effort, I bought a coin separator so that I could sort out the quarters, nickels and dimes. The banks do not take these loose coins and so they all need to be wrapped in their appropriate sleeves. This was a tedious chore but it had to be done so that all the monies could be deposited. As time went by it proved to be a royal pain in the neck.

The toughest part of this business was the actual pay phone location sites and the people there who were using them. Because I had to go to these dubious sites, to collect the monies, I was putting myself in a risky situation. I always felt that I was being watched, by people of dubious character and had to continually watch my back. At first I used to go each Friday morning but I soon realized that I had to randomly change my routine so that no-one could predict when I was coming. When maintaining the phones, which could take an hour or so, I always had a second person with me as a safety measure and the bigger he was, the better. This was to deter anyone from thinking that they could rob or harm me. I must say that my wife, from the very start, was unhappy with this dodgy business and preferred that I would be involved in something a little less dangerous. In spite of all this I never was harmed, in any way, or robbed but I always had an uneasy feeling that something was lurking just around the corner and so caution was the order of the day. I had people try to break into the pay phones, to steal the cash, on several occasions but they only succeeded in breaking phone parts which inevitably cost me money to replace. Another ridiculous ploy was for someone to put a plug coin into the drop box to jamb up the coin slot thus rendering the phone unusable. At some locations I found that someone had actually tampered with the outside wiring by rerouting them to his trailer so that others could use my equipment to make calls from his home phone. This would be someone who was living right next to my phone location and he would charge other people to make their calls from his phone and take my money. It is amazing how ingenious some people are when they have nothing to do all day but think of dishonest ways to make money without even working. Then if they could not steal from me, out of frustration, they would cut the incoming phone line so that no-one else could use it and I was again unable to make money. On quite a few occasions I had to take the pay phone out of a location because of this kind of maltreatment. This was a pity because the decent people living there were deprived of the convenience of this amenity. I persevered with this frustrating pay phone business for three years by which time I recouped all I had invested in them. I then broke them all down, in separate parts, and took all the recyclable metals to the scrap dealer and got a nice cash lump sum which made this bad experience more palatable. Now, at the age of sixty five, I began writing books which has proved to be a much more gracious pastime. My author wife and I work from our home here, on the Gulf Coast of Florida, and could not be more pleased with how our lives have turned out. Because we sell through Amazon our books and e-books are available worldwide.

CHAPTER ELEVEN

The Neanderthal Syndrome

It's official, I am a dinosaur! In other words I am one of the few people, in today's western world, that does not carry a cell phone. This is quite strangely unique in this modern electronic, computerized age and some people will deem me to be a pariah but I stand firm on this issue. I don't behave this way just to be stubborn but because I don't see the point to being at everyone's beck and call for twenty four hours of every day. I have a land line telephone, at home, which has an attached message machine on it, which keeps me in touch with the world at large. However, when I'm out and about I don't want anyone calling me to ask what I am doing or to engage me in idle chat or frivolous gossip. Because they don't have a social life, of their own, it does not mean that I have to give up my time to sympathize with their pathetic situation. Being a writer I really enjoy talking to just about anyone who has a good story to tell. The bits of useful and interesting data that I glean, from these conversations, can be extremely beneficial and therefore I do not want my thought process interrupted. You would be surprised by just how many, of my colorful stories, have been initiated by the interesting people that I converse with and the meaningful details that come to light.

Because of my stance, on this subject, I can stand back objectively and observe the antics of the many people who do, in fact, carry a cell phone no matter where they are or what they are doing. There was a nasty incident at a school recently when a student, during a class, refused to stop using her cell phone and was continually disrupting the whole proceedings. The teacher asked her to cease and when she didn't the Principal was called and she still refused to give up her cell phone. Finally they had to call in a school security guard who, on being refused yet again, ejected the student unceremoniously from the class. The over zealous guard has since been dismissed from his job but none of this would have been necessary if the student had shown reasonability in the first place. A study has recently been released saying that today's children are, without a doubt, addicted to their phones and cannot function in a normal manner without them. I know that many professional people need their phones for many authentic reasons but in numerous circumstances a person does not have to be on call twenty four/seven. As I take my coffee, at a beach café each morning, on many instances I see people's breakfasts being interrupted and, by what I can gather from the conversation, not for any good reason other thank shear boredom on the part of the caller. On other instances, at the café, I will see a young male and female couple individually engrossed in texting on their cell phones and totally ignoring each other. The begs the question as to whether they would answer their phones when engaged in a steamy sexual encounter. I sincerely hope not.

Another aspect to this narcissistic society, which we have become, is the selfie. It appears that most people today cannot get enough experiences to fill their memories and so they have to record every single event with yet another picture of them selves. Pictures of them sitting down, standing up, eating a meal, celebrating with an alcoholic beverage or just about any other conceivable situation. This Eodipus complex, that today's younger people have, has engendered a self adoring generation with a high tendency for instant gratification. I realize that some unique situations, like an amazing sun set or perhaps an elusive dolphin, deserve to be recorded but to snap photographs of every mundane occasion is somewhat redundant. Historic times such as weddings or other family gatherings, particularly with older relatives, should without a doubt be notarized for all to remember. However, some off the cuff snap shots, of no particular importance, would better be disregarded and not emphasized or perpetuated. I hope these observations do not portray me as some kind of a kill joy because I actually enjoy the company of other people as much as the next man. I make my comments because cell phones seem to be sucking the life and ingenuity away from our younger people. It is almost as if they cannot function or survive without their cell phones and God help them if, for whatever reason, the communications infrastructure ever fails. This would bring about a total collapse of around three generations of disenchanted beings. I find myself compelled to watch survivalist type programs, on the television, and I do this to remind myself just how little the human body can live on when extreme conditions are met. I know a young woman who is completely dysfunctional if she does not have her cell phone, her Star Bucks cup of coffee and her cigarettes. What a sad reflection on our modern society!

This epidemic is not prevalent to just America. A year or so ago I was on a visit to the United Kingdom and had to take a train from Newport, Wales to Chester, England a trip of about two hours. I was seated in a booth with a table between me and who ever was to sit opposite. A delightful young lady entered and broadly smiled at me before sitting across the table and I thought what an ideal opportunity for some scintillating conversation. Well I could not have been more wrong because from the time that the train left the station she never looked away from her cell phone. Now it wasn't the case of her reading a prolonged e-book it was that she and some unknown person had a texting conversation for the whole two hours. She would send a message and then wait for the reply and, in turn, would reply to that message and so on, ad nauseam, for the entire afternoon. I looked out of the window and watched so many interesting sights but she missed everything so that she could talk to someone who was not even in the same stratosphere as her. On another occasion I was hosting a business associate to dinner but he continually interrupted the meal to take incoming calls on his cell phone. In the end it took for me to tell him that if he didn't turn off his phone I would leave the restaurant and our business dealings would be permanently curtailed. He suddenly came to his senses and apologized by saying that he was so accustomed in acting this way that he sometime forgets to adopt a sociable attitude. It was then that I realized the many people are programmed to receive a call whether it is important or not. Yes, some professional people such as doctors, attorneys, politicians, etc have to be on top of their jobs at all times. However, the average man in the street must stop kidding himself that every call he gets is world shattering and needs his immediate attention. At best this is narcissistic.

In days gone by children were taught many things so that they could be well informed adults in their later life. All this knowledge was contained in each persons finely tuned brain and on many occasions these facts could be drawn upon and used in their day to day life. The modern generation, however, feels that to learn many of these details is unnecessary because they have them catalogued in their cell phones. This makes individuals less knowledgeable and thus less interesting to be with. To hold a conversation with many of today's younger people is almost like pulling teeth. They have lost the art of meaningful and flowing conversation and if asked to comment, on any given subject, they answer with abrupt and insipid sentences. Yes, they are masters of the cell phone but I sometimes wonder what would happen to them if they found themselves void of their coveted phones. The standard of education has gone down and when asked to put pen to paper, at an old style regular exam, they are flummoxed. Most of today's teenagers cannot correctly spell the majority of words which are comprised of more than five or six letters. Not only is their verbalization impeded but their hand writing is quite appalling with a good number of them not being able to write in cursive English. If two candidates applied to me for a job and one was properly written whereas the other was submitted with chicken scratch scrawl, I know which one I would select to employ. I say this because it is not only the bad writing that lets them down it's the fact that they were too indifferent to try and master the subject. To me this points to their work ethic as being sub-standard and that they don't have the fortitude to knuckle down when things begin to get tough. It is too easy for the new generations to say that they don't need to learn these particular details but so much time is lost, in the business arena, explaining to them things that should be common knowledge. I know that no amount of griping is going to reverse these trends, because this subject is now considered as "fate accompli." Perhaps I am throwing snowballs at the moon, with my disappointment of this state of affairs, because this situation it is unlikely to change any time soon.

In spite of my rhetoric, on this subject, I want to make it clear that we do still have many very talented, independent young people who use cell phones with great skill and fortitude. The sector that I am referring to is those idle minded individuals who use their cell phones as a crutch to make them feel wanted and important. These are mainly the people who instead of making things happen in life, want to be continually updated on what other more resourceful individuals are bringing to fruition. Information has recently also come to light stating that today's average young people spend as much as nine hours a day playing mundane computer games that fail to offer anything vaguely realistic. They lock themselves away, from all other human contact, in idle bids to build imaginary farms or fight imaginary wars. For this they are given imaginary points which supposedly rates the level of ingenuity that they have attained during these idle venture. It is no wonder that a good portion of our younger generations are unable to function effectively in the essentials of life which matter the most. Building a stable career, functioning in an appropriate way with fellow human beings or attaining complete independence from their parents all seem to be too much to ask of them. The pity of all this is that those people, entrenched in this category, have not the slightest inkling that their lives are being wasted. I have two close friends who tell me that video games have destroyed their sons lives.

As a side bar on the modern subject of people wasting their time when texting or communicating with others to satisfy their egos. A recent report has just accentuated the fact that people who use Facebook do so, in the main, to satisfy their own view points on life in general. The report emphasizes the fact that most people seek out facts that confirm their beliefs and ignore contrary information. The study explored Face Book users, between 2010 and 2014, to find out if they accepted opposing views or do they only accept virtual equivalents of their view point. The report uses the term "conspiracy", to describe this phenomenon, that spreads their opinions to be mainly adopted by like minded bloggers. Even if the facts are baseless the conspiracy theories rapidly spread within such communications. More generally Facebook users tend to choose and share stories containing messages that they accept and negate those which they reject. If a story fits with what they believe they are far more likely to spread it and thus is picked up by other like minded people. The concequence is that a proliferation of biased narratives are spread by unsubstantiated rumors, mistrust and paranoia. The study also found that when like minded people speak with one another they tend to end up thinking more extreme versions of what they originally believed. As people accept others , who agree with them, they then become more confident of their original opinions. If people begin with a certain belief and then find information that confirm it, this will intensify their commitment to that very belief and so strengthens the bias. Suppose, for instance, that a person believes that, say, Donald Trump would make a great President. Arriving at this judgement on your own might be tentative. However, after you learn that a lot of people on line agree, you are then more likely to end up with a much greater certainty and have distain for others who don't agree. Wow, another black fly in the Chardonnay!

CHAPTER TWELVE

As The Stomach Turns

I've always thought that my beautiful wife Sharon should have be in Hollywood and just recently I watched her make her debut television appearance. Although this was pre-filmed, several months ago, this was my first time of seeing it, tape delayed, on the small screen. Normally I would be ecstatic but the ridiculous circumstances, that brought this all about, made it a less than pleasant experience. Sharon appeared on the "Judge Judy Show" where people looking for fair play take their grievances in front of the savvy Judge Scheindlin. This lady has been a judge for around forty years and to say that she has been around the block a few times would be a massive under statement. Anyone trying to pull the wool over her eyes is in for a rude awakening as she can see through any disingenuous plea. Sharon's wayward daughter had brought this all about when she invited a guy, who she had just met, to live at the house where her two daughters also resided. It is fare to say that Sharon's daughter has some huge personality problems and, to sum it up, if you put her in a room with one hundred men, she would choose the very worse one there. This particular selection of hers was recently released from prison, thus could not get regular work, and so was flat broke. Now you would think that some red flags would go up, in the daughter's mind, but she dived head long into giving this bum anything that he desired. This action also proved that the daughter has no moral compass. She also had not worked for the best part of a year and so my wife Sharon was paying her rent to ensure the grand children were not rendered homeless.

When the boyfriend was thrust into our family he promised Sharon that he would take on some serious work and begin putting money into the household so that Sharon could step out of her financial burden. Sharon is nearing retirement age and she was hoping that her daughter, for once in her life, could become financially solvent. Now Sharon's daughter has had more jobs than any other person that I have ever met and she has been bounced out of almost most of them because of her weird and unmanageably attitude. All this is part of a personality disorder where her unstable actions end up disrupting everyone else in that work environment. She has no manners, no tact and her dialog is about as subtle as a sledge hammer. It doesn't take too long for her work associates to come to the realization that it is virtually impossible to work with her. This employment pattern, of not having predictable moneys, has also caused her to move her residence, almost every year, so that she can keep one step ahead of her debts. Because of her downward spiral this means that she has to have her phone, water, electricity and anything else she needs to survive, put in other people's names. She continually lives her life one step ahead of the law with her existence teetering on a knife edge. All this makes her life a desperate existence with one bad decision after another and no peace of mind.

So here now is Sharon supporting two dead beats and finally she came to her senses and decides enough is enough and has to stop giving them any more money. Even though her daughter's new love interest promised to find work and pay his way, he didn't and so they were evicted within six months of his arrival. At this point it probably goes without saying that, although they both denied it, there was obviously drugs involved in this pathetic and unholy relationship. Because of the eviction both of Sharon's grand daughters moved on. The eighteen year old went to live with her boy friends family and the eleven year old was court ordered to live with her father. Sharon's daughter, who was drug free before hitching up with the dead beat, went to rehab and the pathetic boy friend moved on to free load off his brother. This now left Sharon to clear out all of her daughter's belongings, from the evicted house, with the help of one man who she paid. Sharon refused to allow me to help because she did not want me to see the deplorable conditions that the house had become since the introduction of the useless wastrel. She then hired a truck and deposited all her daughter's belongings into storage which she is still paying to this very day. All this cost Sharon around $10,000 and not one iota of thanks from her daughter who, in her twisted mind, seems to think that this is all normal.

Sharon, to try and get some money back and not wanting to sue her penniless daughter, decided to take the case to the "Judge Judy Show" in the hope of some compensation. The case was accepted to be televised, on national TV, and so Sharon took her daughter all the way to California in the hope of being awarded $5,000 which is the maximum that the show would allow. Of course, the dead beat was also paid to appear but was booked into a different hotel so no contact, between the parties, would be had before appearing on the program. At this time in the proceedings, Sharon's daughter had been living with us and , as is her usual modus operandi, was not paying one single penny for our kindness. Sharon unfortunately lost the case, as I suspected she would, because Judge Judy deemed that since her daughter had willingly invited the lay-about to co-habitat with her, she had no recourse for any monies to be paid. In other words her daughter's complete stupidity and naivety was so over whelming that it was her fault that the whole ridiculous episode took place. Judge Judy felt a lot of sympathy for Sharon and made the dead beat look totally stupid in front of ten million television viewers but ruled in his favor. In spite of the cunningness of her daughter's, so called, boy friend to seize the opportunity to live free of charge, there was simply nothing that could be done. During the court proceedings Sharon seemed very distracted which is not her usual demeanor and this was because as she was leaving the hotel, to go to the show, she could not find her wallet. Obviously this threw her concentration for a loop because the wallet contained all her credit cards, I.D. and money. When she returned from the show it had been miraculously found, by the maid service, secreted under the bed in her hotel room.

What Sharon did not know was that one of her credit cards was missing and when she returned home to Florida the credit card company contacted us. They reported that the card had been used, throughout the Los Angeles area, for taxi fares, food and other miscellaneous items. Would you believe that, after all Sharon had gone through to straighten her daughter's life out, it was she who stole the credit card. She had selfishly taken the card, in a criminal act, so that she could meet with the dead beat boy friend. Like a snake in the grass she had secretly met with him the night before and the night of the show by lying to her mother and in her twisted mind this was all completely acceptable. She had slept with the enemy and disrespected her own mother so that she and her worthless boyfriend could share a honeymoon together in California, once more at someone else's expense. Her cold and calculating plot had once again been at the cost of the only person, in the universe, that cared a damn for her. In days of yore when a person leaked information to the enemy, or was caught fraternizing, they were called a traitor and then summarily executed.

Immediately Sharon and her daughter returned to our house, from L A , she packed her bags and quickly left for God knows where. She had obviously been using her mother just to get her through yet another rough period of her life and now that her love life was back on track, it was time to move on. She convinced other people to allow her to live with them but as soon as she was entrenched she would deviously also try to slide in the deadbeat. Each time she tried this devious ploy, she was unceremoniously thrown out but then she found someone who would take the dead beat with her but that only lasted a month. Their hosts came home one day and found him shooting up heroin, even though he insisted that he was now clean, and so he was once again kicked to the curb. These kind people had recently lost their own son, to the very same drug, yet the delusional daughter had the audacity to introduced another druggie into their home. They were so keen to get rid of him that, out of their own pockets, they bought him a one way ticket back to Oklahoma where it is reported that he came from. They personally drove him to the airport and put him on a fast plane out of town. Now that he is hopefully out of the picture she comes around her mother and I and wants to act like the whole affair was some frivolous and laughable event. She still does not understand that she plotted and deceived to get her own needs satisfied and, in so doing, prevented her mother from recouping part of the money that was kindly and lovingly loaned to her. To think that all this upheaval was caused by the action of one selfish persons who, without thought for any of her other family members, made a rash and absolutely ridiculous decision. What a callous and selfish excuse for a human being she has turned out to be.

So Sharon's debut television appearances turned out to be far from the happy occasion which she had hoped for. Her daughter's devious plans had secretly blown her hopes out of the water with the trip to California being a complete disaster. At one time I thought of accompanying them but I am now glad that I didn't because there would have been one less passenger in the plane on the return flight. There is an old adage which says that if you fool me once its shame on you but if you fool me twice, then its shame on me. Sharon, God bless her, is still trying to straighten her daughter's life out but, with this young woman, I'm afraid that history is bound to repeat itself. She has a no-toriously short memory and I suspect that the events, that she herself caused, have already faded into oblivion. My dread is that as soon as Sharon's re-establishes her daughter, at her next living quarters, she will telephone Oklahoma and the dead beat will come speeding back for another round of free loading. My only hope is that in the interim the dead beat will hook up with a new patsy and decide to stay there and sponge off her. I love my wife dearly and it vexes me to see her daughter treat her like some money lender who is never to be repaid. After all the kind-ness that she has given, to this thankless cause, she deserves to be treated better than this. This daughter, who has crossed the line morally, ethically and criminally, now expects us to renew our trust her. Only time will tell.

Incidentally, when this show was televised Sharon watched it at a party with some of her close girl friends so that they could all see the injustice of this episode. Needless to say the two villainous dead beats were appropriately booded at every given opportuni-ty and it was obvious, to all, just who the villains of the story were. This was the only scant satisfaction that Sharon received in return for all the kindness she has continually shown to her wayward daughter.However, a week after the show aired Sharon received an unexpected hand written letter from an unknown person who lives in Rochester, New York. How he got our address is a mys-tery but he wrote to empathized with Sharon's mistreatment. The letter at first seemed harmless but as it went on it appeared to be something other than a letter of mere support. It ended with the sender's cell phone number and a request for Sharon to contact him. Isn't life strange when love and respect, which should have come from her daughter, emerged from a total stranger who has never met the subject of his desire. There is no accounting for the unscrupulous workings of a sick mind and I never cease to be amazed by the evil deeds that it can visit upon others.

CHAPTER THIRTEEN

A Blight On The Lands

Although I am not a devout Christian, who goes to a church and participates in Sunday sermons and other congregational activities, I still pride myself as being a caring person who tries to do good when the need arises. Back in Wales I was a practicing Christian up until the age of around fifteen when some of the things, that I was expected to believe, became questionable and no longer rang true. However, some of the ethics taught to me, during my early church days, still lingers in the back of my mind. Therefore, whenever I witness something that screams for help, without due process, I will step up to the plate and assist when and where I can. The one major thing that has always puzzled me is that there are so many different religions, and also so many additional sects of those specific religions, whose followers sincerely believe that their version of religion is the only true creed in the entire world. Unfortunately because of their belief they feel that they can rightly persecute any other people who do not agree with their rigid ideology.

Around the world the Muslims persecute the Christians, the Buddhists persecute the Muslims, the Hindus persecute the Sikhs and so on and so on. Then within specific religions the Protestants persecute the Catholics and the Sunni persecute the Shiite and many other instances too many to mention. So where does religion end and human kindness and caring become the standard?

From what I understand, from speaking to quite a few experts, nowhere in any of all these religions does the scriptures definitively say that their followers must go out and harm anyone that does not agree with their doctrine. No-one has ever been given this divine right so why, throughout history, do these religions persecute each other to the extent of trying to obliterate others, from the face of the earth, who they consider to be non-believers of their faith. This has been occurring for as long as people have been writing historical records and most probably even before that. From my history lessons, as a child back in Wales, I learned of the Romans persecuting the Jews and Christians, and of the holy conflict between Christians and Muslims. I learned of the English civil war which, unlike the latter one in the USA, was a religious war between Protestants and Catholics. More recently the same two opponents fought again in Northern Ireland and although it was supposed to be a war of independence the foes were again split on religious lines. So looking at this anomaly one can only draw the conclusion that it is man's total misinterpretation, of previous religion's historical events, that is the fatal flaw in his beliefs. Once these atrocities are recorded, as historical fact, next there comes the retaliations for passed events which have been repeated for centuries. For short periods of time all is rosy in the Garden of Eden but once again, for often unclear reasons, the old religious contempt boils over and starts yet other wars purely for secular revenge.

All of the past religious wars have mostly been confined to individual countries and even to regions of countries but now, in 2015, we have seen the emergence of a religious war which one of the contestants has deliberately made into a world wide conflict. ISIS, is a Sunni sect of Muslims that has unlawfully seized a portion of land which encompasses parts of northern Syria and

Iraq. They have set up an independent Caliphate which they want to be a land for their religious sect alone. All the previous inhabitance, of that specific region, had three options. One, to be killed in one of many gruesome ways which includes beheading. Two, they must leave the region, never to return, and everything that they own is plundered, with no compensation. Three, they can stay when allowed and pay taxes to the new regime and obey Sharia law which basically means returning to the days of the dark ages. This strict set of laws means that a thief can have his hand cut off for stealing, woman's clothing must fully cover their bodies or they can be openly flogged on the spot and any unfaithful married persons can be stoned to death, in the streets, by a barbaric mob. I S I S has set up their own government which is funded by the afore said taxes, monies from kidnapping ransoms and by stealing and selling ancient artifacts from treasured historic sights. They have also destroyed many ancient historic sites, throughout the Middle East, because in their Neanderthal minds if these sites existed before the time of the prophet Mohamed they must be contrary to their religion. Their main funding source, however, comes from looting the oil industry which they have taken over, by force, to sell on the black market. This enterprise alone nets billions of illegal moneys for their coffers which they use to fund the buying of arms to keep their armies supplied. They have spread such terror and mayhem throughout that region that around a million people have left to various parts of Europe, rather than stay and live by the terms set by this diabolical and murderous regime. This suits I S I S just fine as they do not want to feed, or care for, anyone who is not totally committed to their manic brand of religion and vicariously spreads their brand throughout Europe.

For the first time in history one sadistic religious group of people can reach out and recruit followers, from all over the world, to their fanatical cause. The electronic computer age was heralded as the savior of mankind but I S I S has used this very media to cause carnage around the world. Before all this many people, from this now unofficial region, traveled to European countries for a better standard of living but not all of them became successful. Because of this there is a small percentage of disenchanted younger men who, for no other reason than being disgruntle, have latched onto the propaganda which I S I S is distributing. Their lawless edict is "Come back to your home land and fight with us and when we win you will be rewarded." For almost two years the western world stood back and watched in the hope that the neighboring countries, around the Caliphate, would go in and take care of this intolerable situation. When they did not the western world decided it was time to act and became involved particularly with the introduction of air bombing raids. These strikes were specific in their targeting and destroyed many vital assets, of the bogus regime, such as oil installations, command posts and telecommunication centers. Drone air strikes also targeted and killed a good number of the top ranking officials of the new, so called, Caliphate. I S I S now, for the first time, is feeling the strains of war and has reached out to those disenchanted young men who are already living in foreign countries which are now performing those bombing raids. Basically their message is to not come to the Middle East to join them but stay at home and contrive to kill as many harmless civilians by any means possible. There favorite method of killing is to wear an explosive device and walk into a crowded area and detonate their bomb. To kill unarmed non-combatants, often women and children, who are merely going about their daily lives and not causing harm to anyone, is a most cowardly, cold hearted and a inhuman act of terrorism. They have been indoctrinated that somewhere in the Koran it says that male martyr will go to heaven where forty virgins will be awaiting them. I wonder what female martyrs get? I hope they go there sooner than planned but instead end up in hell where their souls will eternally burn for their sins.

These heretics have committed such horrific crimes in numerous countries around the world but their three most recent, that of downing a Russian plane and the Paris and Brussels attacks, has galvanized these countries. An all out war will now take place in their illegally formed state, the likes of which they could never imagine. Justice will prevail for all those displaced and murdered individuals. At this point I must state that when it comes to the ground fighting which has gone on, almost unnoticed over the passed two years, the Kurds have been the most heroic and affective fighters. It is my humble opinion that when this whole situation is finally resolved, and lands are divided up, the Kurds should be given their own autonomous country. I realize that Turkey and Iran will be loathed to do so but, because of their bravery, at least Syria and Iraq, who the Kurds have been helping, should cede their portions to these brave Peshmerga fighters. In a clever ploy the Kurds have formed a unit of trained women snipers, to combat these invaders, as to be killed by a female will greatly offend the I S I S misguided ethic.

For the first time, in recorded history, we have a fanatical religious sect who will kill anyone who does not abide by their absurd ideology. Although they are Sunnis they will even kill other Sunnis who are members of a different sect of that same religion. In other words they have zero tolerance for any human being who does not adhere to their primitive and rigorous Sharia laws. They want to impose, on other people, a standard of living that has its roots way back in the sixth century and it is so out of date, that it is impossible to comprehend living in such a manner. Not only that, they want to spread their backward thinking around the world and there is no tolerance for anyone refusing to accept it. They will line up groups of people and execute them en masse. Not since the Nazi regime, which caused World War II, has such a callous and unrelenting group of people been allowed to roam the earth. For the first two years, of their ugly existence, no moderate Islamic group leaders would speak out against this barbarous bunch of killers. Now, after a million people have been killed and a further million have been driven out, from this region of discontent, finally in the mosques the Imams are now preaching the message that these people are nothing more then murderous thugs. They are a blight upon our otherwise sublime world and the sooner that we completely eradicated these radicals, the better life will be for every other living thing. It is time for a combined and systematic assault to be leveled, against this horrific bunch of misfits, so that the world can return to the happy times that we all enjoyed before their ominous shadow darkened the earth. The sooner that this is done the better for all concerned and I, for one, cannot wait to see the total annihilation of these fanatics become a reality. No single religion should ever be allowed to take complete control over all others. Freedom of religion has been a corner stone of America's basic democratic ideology and no other misguided group of heathens will ever be allowed to destroy this principal. We have tolerated the existence of their lunatic dogma, for long enough, and it is time to help them meet their ancestors which, incidentally, they seem to think is their God given destiny.

In the past few days, that it has taken me to compile this very chapter, a huge historic event has taken place. Pope Francis, the leader of the world's catholic religion, has made a much heralded visit to the African countries of Kenya, Uganda and the conflict wracked country of the Central African Republic where, once again, there is war between Christians and Muslims. Pope Francis was born in relative poverty and, unlike many of his predecessors, seems to be more in touch with the basic woes of the average man. As I have previously stated, I am not a practicing Christian and I have never been a Catholic but I admire this man. On the last day of his visit he asked to attend the biggest mosque in the Centrals badly divided capitol of Bangui. There he appealed to the Imams, of that country, to preach that religion can never justify violence. This brave and sincere appeal will not affect the world domination plans of I S I S but perhaps the Imams can dissuade young Muslim men from joining the carnage which they want to spread throughout the world. If temperate Muslim people can preach the path of peace and forgiveness, and instill this into their agitated young men, they might abandon these tyrannical traits.

Just recently several disenchanted I S I S converts have crossed back over and surrendered to Allied forces. The ideology, of this diabolical band of thugs, is so radical and barbaric that these current deserters could no longer tolerate or justify living under such an extreme regime. This might herald the beginning of the decline and hopefully the disappearance of probably the most hated fanatical group known to mankind. Why our current President refuses to identify them, as being an Islamic terrorist group, is way beyond reasonable belief. I am positive that the next elected President, whoever he or she might be, will not be so ineptly inclined. Hopefully this is the thin end of the wedge and perhaps many more disenchanted rebels will follow by laying down their arms and return to a more civilized mode of life style. Hallelujah!

CHAPTER FOURTEEN
Glory Days

The other day I was idly listening to the car radio when a song came on that really started me thinking. The song was Glory Days by Bruce Springsteen and the lyrics explained how whenever he met old school pals they immediately would reminisce about their younger days when they enjoyed life the most. The Boss's lyrics was about how, when people get older, they only remember the successful achievements and occasions from when they were in their prime. They hardly ever remember or mention the naïve, stupid or misguided events from their past. In summation they would invariably say that those times were the best days of their lives. I too have sometimes been guilty of approaching this subject, of times gone by, in a similar manner but recently I have had to reverse my thinking. The reason for this change of heart is that my present life style has surpassed, by far, anything that I have previously experienced. For the past sixteen years I have been living in what, in my humble opinion, is positively a most memorable location of the entire world. I share this experience with one of the most loving and beautiful woman that it has been my pleasure to have ever met in my meandering life. I have previously had many memorable times and occasions but here in this place, at this point in time, I have never been happier. The climate, here in Florida, the flora and fauna, the food, the entertainment and the generous people are all exceptional and it is extremely difficult to think of just one aspect, of life, that is disagreeable. Time seems to move at the speed of a glacier and these last sixteen years of my life have, without a doubt, been my Glory Days and I say this without reservation or hesitation.

In my previous times in Wales, England and Michigan I have had some exceptional times at my employment, at sporting events and during all my travels. In Wales I won a Junior Rugby Cup, a Welsh Boys Clubs three mile race against national competition and had many good and loyal friends. I had girl friends galore, throughout a ten mile radius of my home town, so my life was a filled with much happiness and contentment. In Cheshire, England, now weighing a hundred and sixty pounds, my rugby flourished and I became a well known figure in the North West region and was recognized almost everywhere. In every team that I played for I wore the number ten shirt which meant that I dictated the style of play and tactics to ensure a win. Many years later, on a visit to Wales a friend of mine told me that he had ran into one of my early rugby coaches. This man said to my friend "If Lyn Clarke would have stayed in Wales he would have played for Wales." What an enormous compliment! My summer time track racing was another successful pastime where I won many awards and gifts. At the same time I expanded my social activities which brought many other good friends. No matter where I went I was always recognized as a person of note and my reputation spread throughout that area. My job, as a Sales Engineer, took me virtually all over Britain and occasionally to Sweden, Germany and France with the bonus of these trips being paid for by my employer. During this period of my life the dating scene was exotic with some of the most hauntingly gorgeous young European women and hearts torn in every which way.

I then moved on to Michigan, in America, where my work related life continued as before but within a much larger sphere. My job as a Sales Engineer took me far and wide and the women I met just couldn't get enough of me. I was now playing soccer with a scrappy bunch of Scottish, Irish, Welsh and English guys who were uncompromising on and off the field of play. Again, I was always in the lime light and although not exactly famous, I was still highly notable and had enormous fun and excitement wherever I went. I also made a point of attending a good number of musical shows and concerts and seemed never short of exciting things to do. While in America I made a point of returning to the United Kingdom, usually once a year, to linked up with past friends for some social revelry. I had many fabulous times and no-one could ever say that my life was dull, in fact, it was down right crazy. The major difference between then and here in Florida, is that although exciting and memorable events previously occurred a good number of times, my joy and zest for life now occurs every day. Daily events are so exhilarating that sometimes I cannot wait to go to bed so I can wake up and see what adventures the new day will bring. Almost always I wake up to sunshine and I can walk outside, onto my front porch, wearing the minimum of clothing and the weather is already warm and pleasant. The birds are singing and the scent of flowers fill the air making where I live a paradise from the early morning on. Apart from the garden birds, because I live one hundred yards from the beach, many sea birds such as the pelicans are also up and flying about in search of breakfast. Then there are the birds of prey like the bald eagles, the ospreys and the turkey vultures which are, by now, also on the wing. The air seems to be alive, with a thousand sights and sounds, from the moment the sun rises and this brings immediate gratification on an enormous scale. The warm weather also brings wellness and a type of self awareness that accompanies good health and I have hardly had, no more than, a few days of being unwell in all the years that I have lived here. The mixture of good health and happiness is exhilarating but I must give due warning that too much sun can be counter productive. Because I love working with all the trees, plants, flowers and landscaping projects, in my yard, I have to be aware not to do so during the hottest times of the day. To ensure that my skin remains well I visit a dermatologist twice a year, for a full body examination, to make sure that nothing untoward has presented it self.

Because of the climate and the beautiful surrounds, on this island, people who live or visit here are rarely ever in a bad mood. This tropical island seems to bring the best out of everyone and so good fellowship is part and parcel of a typical day on Anna Maria Island. Whenever a visitor crosses any of the three bridges, leading onto this island, a magical transformation takes place. Their pace of life slows down perceptibly as they sub-consciously become aware that they have entered a place of almost religious tones and their attitude of mind becomes calm. Because the pace of life seems to move at the speed of a glacier, they too drive slower than usual because they want to ensure that they don't miss any significant sight. Whether it is a bikini clad sun tanned shapely young lady crossing the road or an exotically colored bird flying by. The people here have broad smiles on their faces and are polite and kind to all others whether locals or strangers. Visitors are eager to join in the ambiance and life style of our island residence and will strike up friendly conversations at the drop of a hat. Almost everyone you meet here has a friendly disposition and appears hale and hearty which helps to spread the elusion that this is the idyllic place to live. This location is a magnet which attracts many artistically inclined people such as writers, painters, sculptors, weavers and all sorts of jewelry makers. For retired people these artistic items can be bought or sold at numerous open air markets and provide a good second source of income which I, for one, take full advantage of. What a bonus Mother Nature has provided.

When we talk about the quality of life there is one aspect that we often take for granted. I am referring to personal safety and peace of mind. There is no value that can physically be accredited to this asset of life but I feel it is worth a fortune. Once again I must mention the events, of today's modern culture, where murder and mayhem seemed to have become the accepted normal for the world. We sometimes take our usual peaceful life style for granted but when unknown people come into our neighborhood, to do harm and misdeeds, it is then that our safety is abruptly disrupted. Although I have seen hard times in my life I have never faced physical threats to my well being and I hope I never have to. To live in a safe haven, whether it be house, town, city or country, gives an extreme sense of calmness. It is only when this foundation is shaken that we ever give it any mind at all. I am so lucky because here, on Anna Maria Island, we are somewhat isolated from the main stream of modern misfortunes. Yes, we do have some criminal activities here but compared with what is going on, in the rest of the world, these are minor. For a small seven mile long island we have a police force here for each of the three separate cities. Apart from this level of security another factor, which dissuades criminals from coming here for their dishonest activities, is that the only access is over one of three draw bridges. In the case of a villainous act all the police have to do is tell the bridge tenders to raise the central spans of bridges and they are prevented from leaving. You can never completely eradicate petty crime and we do have a class of boat living people who seem to get into their fare share of minor crimes. Also being a warm tropical paradise we have a smattering of homeless people who make their way here, particularly during the winter months, to set up camp on the beach. However, our police are well versed to dealing with these petty nuisances and so these incidents are just a hiccup in the normal trend of our existence and are barely noticeable. Push bikes quite often go missing but in a lot of cases the are found leaning against a tree or in some foreign bike rack and, in most cases, are returned to the owner. On the physical assault side, of the equation, there has been minimal incidents. These usually involve fist fights between drunken partiers, but never amount to much and are soon quelled. When I see what is going on in the Middle Eastern countries and the attacks by terrorist, on major cities around the world, I am supremely glad that I reside in this delightful yet remote little spot on the Gulf of Mexico. I feel so sorry for those people, from around the world, who now have to live in constant fear for their lives. I hope, one day soon, that they will all, once more, feel as safe and contented as I do. I will continue to sing the praises of living here in the Sun Shine state of Florida. The warm climate has many benefits for the welfare of the inhabitants both human and animal alike. The beauty and scents of the indigenous trees and plants are intoxicating and are a pleasure to the senses. The climate is healthy because of the abundance of clear, fresh air. The beaches are some of the most beautiful on this planet Earth and the water, that laps upon them, is warmly inviting and quite surreal. The abundance of birds and fish is truly amazing and even the reptiles are friendly so long as they are treated with respect. The skies are a wonder to behold, particularly at sun rise and sun set, and they are so clear that a person can literally see for miles in any direction. All this adds up to a life of contentment for the lucky inhabitants here who are blessed and enjoy good health with a generous portion of happiness.

Having lauded all these advantages there is yet one more, that should not be omitted, and this is the eye popping vibrant and vivid colors which are enhanced by our bright sunshine. Of the birds the pure snowy white of the egrets and herons, the shocking pink of the roseate spoonbills. The bright green of the flitting parrots, the deep orange of the tanagers and the cobalt blue of the indigo bunting, just to name a few. Of the plants the luscious purple of the wisteria. The reds, yellows and whites of the hibiscus bushes and frangipani trees. The deep red of the oleander trees and the deep yellow of the daffodil trees. An added advantage is that all these colors, and many more, can be witnessed in unison which offers a magnificent array of sights. This collage of beautiful colors brightens up the lives of we lucky in-habitants who reside here in this idyllic place. All this, plus the multitude of brightly colored fishes, has to be seen to be believed as it is simply exhilarating. We also have a two mile long sister island, just half a mile to the north of us, call Egmont Key. This has a light house, a bird and tortoise sanctuary and the ruins and of the two hundred year old Fort Dade which once guarded the mouth of Tampa Bay. The grave yard there is of interest to historians as the island was once used to house people that had yellow fever back in the late 1800's. A beautiful spot to enjoy the peace and tranquility of a sun filled afternoon. You should get there fast and then take it slow.

So there you have it, my glory days are now. I have worked the wonder lust out of my system and my life is now in order. I no longer need to be in the lime light although, on this island, I am still well respected. I have a beautiful, talented and loyal woman who keeps me happy in every possible way. My home is fully paid for and I am debt free. I can financially afford, within reason, almost anything that I want. I am in excellent health for a man of my age and I still play soccer twice a week. I have many good and generous friends who can truly be re-lied upon, for assistance, at any given time. My surrounds are breath taking and every day is a new adventure. My existence is now better than ever and each day is filled with wonder-ful sights and experiences. I feel completely safe and content-ed and walk around with a song in my heart, a swagger in my step and a smile on my face. When I pass on to the other side, I sincerely hope that heaven is my destination. If this happens I will be one of a minority group of people who have been for-tunate enough to have be in heavenly surrounds twice. What more could any man wish for?

CHAPTER FIFTEEN

Our World Is Changing

Apart from my glowing report of life, here on earth, there is one dark and ominous cloud on the horizon which I feel compelled to mention although this slow but inevitable change of weather patterns will not drastically affect my lifetime. This is the phenomenon called global warming which, whether man made or natural, is going to alter the lives of millions people on this planet if present industrial trends are not contained. Recently there has been a multinational worldwide top level meeting to stem the pollution which causes this problem and although there was a unanimous agreement, to take measures to address this doomsday scenario , for now the madness still prevails. At the increasing rate, of our planet warming, the ocean's waters will rise and many low lying countries will be swamped and ultimately devastated. Many island states will disappear entirely while other countries will see large swaths of their lands significantly reduced. For people living at higher altitudes, global warming is not a pressing problem but for people like me, living barely six feet above sea level, this will bring a staggering amount of despair and hardships to our lives. The increased heat over the oceans will produce bigger and more destructive hurricanes and monsoons. The Artic and Antarctic ice fields are melting and glaziers all over the world will diminish. The increased cold water in the oceans could reverse the warm Gulf Stream and this will present a much chillier climate. for many northern areas of the globe. The increased temperatures over the lands will bring greater and more devastating tornadoes, forest fires, flash floods and subsequently landslides. More earthquakes and volcano eruptions will occur and even the migration patterns of birds will be altered. Incidentally, the Christmas season of 2015, in most parts of America, had no snow and temperatures around 70F degrees. The average temperatures, for the whole of that year, is the highest ever recorded since 1883 and is thus the warmest known to man. In Florida we have experienced tornadoes in January and up in the northern States the bears did not hibernate until later than usual. All these drastic weather changes will eventually bring about a sad increase in deaths, plagues and illnesses and will eventually cause a drastic reduction of the world's population.

These extreme conditions will affect people even if they live in multilevel home. They can abandoned the ground floor of their houses but the streets, around them, will still remain under water. All their landscaped yards will be destroyed with most plants being killed off by the invading salt water. Apart from the fish and sea birds all other wild animals will instinctively move to higher for drier lands in search of food and habitat. If some people stubbornly decide to keep living in these conditions they will have to use boats, to get to dry land, when they need to go shopping for food and other essentials. House pets will present another problem because they will be home bound and not able to exercise properly as previously. Farm animals such as cows, sheep and pigs will have to be relocated so that we can maintain our expected level of meat supplies. Municipal services, such as garbage collection, will be virtually impossible unless it is undertaken with the use of sea going barges. The affect on emergency services like police, ambulances and fire engines will be just as confusing and disrupted. Under ground gas and electrical supply lines will eventually deteriorate and have to be rebuilt above ground. The problems will be enormous and far too many to be addressed in this narrative but, in a nut shell, if this happens human life styles will be adversely affected for many years to come. The costs of all the additional preventive measures, to combat this mayhem, will cripple a good number of the poorer nations. The lack of grain crops, in the less fortunate countries, will cause starvation, diseases, illnesses, and eventually increased death. These levels will not have been seen, on this Earth, since the Black Death of the middle ages. Like Noah's flood it will be an event of biblical proportions and the world will be permanently altered for endless centuries to come.

If this phenomenon is a natural cycle the seas will eventually drop again, if the fates allow, and one day return to their normal levels but not for an extended period of time. This return to the normality of usual sea levels will be a change for the better but the people, of our current generations, will not be privileged enough to witness this reverse of fortune. Let us all hope that countries that use fossil fuels to energize their industrial production, like the main offender China, will come to their senses and obey this new international agreement and reduce their level of polution. At present it is so high, in Beijing, that the citizens there cannot leave their homes on designated days and must wear face masks, because of dense smog, when they do. Motorists there can only drive every other day and if this is not an omen of things to come, I don't know what is. In Mongolia the grasslands where the herders used to graze their flocks has become a vast desert with the grasses having almost completely disappeared. Beneath the oceans the warmer waters have also begun to slowly destroy the beautiful coral reefs which provides the living habitat for thousands of specimens of fish which are relied upon as a food source for many sea going peoples of the world. Don't forget that around the year 900 AD, in Central America, a thirty year drought completely wiped out the Mayan civilization of approximately twenty million people. This was mainly due to their mismanagement of the land when they cleared the jungle of trees so that they could use the land to grow crops. This change rain patterns and eventually brought about inter city warfare as they fought over what little water remained and eventually their whole civilization collapsed and they disappeared from the earth. This illustrates precisely the fine balance in which the world exists and an increase of only a couple of degrees, in temperature, can bring devastating consequences to the world at large. Future generations will have to endure these unpredictable times.

History has shown that mankind can at least contain this problem if not almost totally resolved it. In Europe, during the nineteenth and early twentieth century's, we underwent the Industrial Revolution and the main source of energy, used back then, was coal. Even as a young lad, growing up during the 1950's and 60's, I remember the smoke stacks of industry billowing out thick black smoke. There were days when the smog, that this condition produced, was so thick that it was difficult to see just ten yards away in any direction. The river, that ran down through my home town, was called the Avon Llewydd which translated from Celtic means gray river. By the time I was a teenager it could be called the black river from the coal dust that had settled in it. Back then not a single fish was to be found in that cesspit of water but now there are trout in the river once more. Many of the men working, down at the coal face died later, in their thousands, from black lung caused by the coal dust which they inhaled. Their lungs would slowly fill up with the dust which made breathing difficult and they eventually suffocated from this terrible ailment. If a coal miner cut himself while under ground, and did not have it properly tended to, the wound would heal itself but leave a permanent black scar caused by the coal dust inside it. When a mountain, piled with coal slag, slid down into the town of Aberfan, in the Rhondda Valley, it buried an elementary school and wiped out a whole generation of young children. Apart from climate conditions these are just a few of the adverse side affects of relying on fossil fuel as a main energy supply. Back then strict laws were enacted, against industrial pollution, and after around thirty years, of stringent enforcement, the air in my country is back to being clear and sweet to breath.

Back when I was growing up we were uninformed about the results of our misdeeds but now we must heavily increase investments into alternative sources of clean energy such as wind and solar. After all, mother nature provides these sources free of charge and we just have to learn how to harness them efficiently. It is no exageration to say that we must, once more, immediately begin to combat this problem. Otherwise other generations, of mankind in years to come, will curse and blame our generation as being blindly stupid for ignoring the worsening of such a drastic climatic event. Our legacy will forever be that we were the generation who did not care enough to keep this amazing planet in good shape. I hate to have commented on such a gloom and doom topic, and what will happen if we all don't come to our senses, but this set of circumstances is something that we have to acknowledge as world changing and not in a good way. As I have already said, during the present my life is wonderful and I expect to have long passed on before this affront, to man's existence, becomes corrected. I hope to God that in the years to come people, here on earth, will be able to enjoy this world as much as I have. However if we, as human beings, do not take this situation seriously and carry on with our wayward habits, there will be a debt to pay and the outcome will not at all be pleasantly received by those who follow in the years to come.

While I am playing the Devil's advocate, the citizens of Flint, Michigan deserve to have lead free water as normally expected.

TELL IT LIKE IT IS

The decision to change the source of their water supply, for cost saving reasons, was short sighted and ill advised. In years gone by General Motors used to make cars in Flint and the water in Mexico was not drinkable. Now, in a fickle quirk of fate, these situations are reversed. What is the world coming to?

CHAPTER SIXTEEN

To Have Or Have Not. That Is The Question

For those readers, who live outside of the United States, the ownership of guns has always been a complicated and puzzling topic of conversation. To people who have been brought up in a society, where fire arms are not allowed, this has always been a bone of contention. It is difficult for someone who has never held a gun, let alone fired one, to fathom out why they would be necessary at all but circumstances here in America are somewhat different. It has to be remembered that when the Pilgrim Fathers landed, at Plymouth Rock, they were appropriately armed so that they could survive by fending off hostiles and hunting for food. If it had not been for this fact it is extremely doubtful that they would have been able to survive. Every day was a battle as they had to prevent starvation, stave off wild beasts and acts of bravery to deter attacks from savage Indians. The settlement in Jamestown, in the Carolinas, ran out of powder and consequently perished. As the inhabited lands became more crowded, with new immigrants, some of the earlier settlers decide to move further west and here again their guns became essential for their well being. This fact is the reason for the West being tamed.

For the previously stated reasons guns became even more important to the point that they were carried and loaded at all times. The new residents had learned, from experience, that one never knew what perils could be faced at any given moment. In many instances not having a gun, at your disposal, could mean certain death as danger lurked around every corner. As the settlers foraged further and further west so did their fire arms and, for their well being, this was an accepted necessity. Because guns were spread far and wide, in massive quantities, in advance of basic laws being enacted, to prohibit them was like closing the barn door after the horse had bolted. As the new settlers became faced with continuous threats of war, from native Indian tribes, they requested for "The Right to Bear Arms" legally. This Second Amendment of 1791 was added to the Constitution and it also enabled militias to be quickly formed to fend off any future intrusions. This after winning their independence from Britain just fifteen years earlier. This same controversial amendment remains in law, to this very day, and is what gun activist always fall back on when the subject of gun control ever arises.The settlement of the States of America, from the Atlantic to the Pacific Oceans, would not have been possible without the availability of fire arms. I realise that, even as near back in time as around a hundred years ago, disputes were settle in the main street at noon with hand guns. Yes, frequently guns have been misused but the question still remains if you were confronted by a criminal or terrorist, who had a gun, which scenario would you opt for. The one where you are helpless and unarmed or the one where you also have a gun at your disposal which puts you in a position to defend yourself.

At this juncture I should announce that only one time, in my entire life, did I ever fire a gun. At the age of fourteen I was visiting a school pal of mine who lived out in the country and he encouraged me to give it a try. The gun was only a pellet rifle which my friend used to kill the over abundance of rats that thrived around where he lived. I brought the loaded rifle up to my eye and scoped all three hundred and sixty degrees of the entire surrounds. I spotted a song bird, singing its tiny heart out, in a tree about sixty yards away and I remember thinking that I had very little chance of hitting it from this range. I fired and, to my horror and dismay, the tiny bird ceased singing and fell to the ground dead. In an instant I was simply shocked to the core and stunned that I had, for no good reason, taken the life of an innocent little creature. The finality of this random event has stayed with me for the whole of my life and, needless to say, I have never handle a fire arm since that morbid occasion. That was about sixty years ago and I can remember my tragic blunder as if it was yesterday. Having seen the consequences, of this thoughtless action, it made me wonder how anyone could, in good conscience, level a gun, at another human being, and fire. I suppose if I had to save the life of a loved one, during a threat of imminent danger, I could but for any other reason I cannot imagine me doing so. Of course, I have always lived in a somewhat civilized surrounds and have never felt the necessity to have a gun for my protection. There are, however, many parts of the USA, to this date in time, where it would be extremely unwise to go without a fire arm and people, from those areas, are used to owning and frequently firing guns. If faced with the meerest hint of danger, these wilderness people would not think twice about using a fire arm in their defence. Basically people, like me, who rarely if ever face danger would argue that guns are not necessary but people who are used to facing danger, on an almost daily basis, will say that they cannot survive without them. In other words I feel that we should not ban guns because, in times of peril, some people's needs are much more important than mine. That basically is it and I expect the situation to stay this way 'til hell freezes over.

Now everything that I have expressed, so far, have been base on normal and expected circumstances in the modern day world. However, in the past two years the whole world's thinking has changed as a group of Islamic terrorist have decided to export their unconventional brand of warfare. They have taken their radical and fervent ideology outside of their home land and have been attacking unarmed people in Africa, Indonesea, France, Britain, America and many other places of the western world. This now brings a new and different view point to the discussion of gun control. Since this cowardly band of thugs only attack soft security spots, where only unarmed people are present, we now have to reconsider the prior views on this subject. I remenber that during my time of living near Detroit, Michigan an armed band of men tried to rob a bar owned by a friend of mine. As they got out of their car it could clearly be seen, on the security monitor from outside, that they were armed and their intentions were not going to be friendly. Unknown to them the bar was a favorite watering hole, of some policemen from Detroit's sixth precinct, and they had seen that the intruders were armed and dangerous. As the robbers boldly entered the bar, brandishing their guns, they were cautioned to halt but being surprised they opened fire. They were met with a hale of bullets as the policemen replied from their vantage points. It was all over in two minutes and the end result was that all the felons were unceremoniously carried out in body bags.

This makes me wonder just how many innocent lives could be saved, in similar situations, if the people being assaulted were fore warned and armed. I also wonder how these unscrupulous terrorist would react if they knew, before planning an attack, that their targets were not just lambs to be slaughtered. The fact that they could expect to face a determine group of people, who had everything they needed to repel them without mercy, may have deterred them. I believe these horrible, misguided radicals are basically cowards and don't have the stomach to face armed combatants when it becomes a fare fight. Times have to change and we can no longer tolerate for the outcome to remain in favor of the villains. People who previously were adamantly against civilians owning fire arms must now rethink this dilemma. They should ponder "What if I were on the subway, or eating at a restaurant, or in the theatre with my loved ones or friends, when terrorists opened fire. In such an event I would prefer to be armed and so protect myself and, if possible, to kill those who are trying to kill me." This is a whole new ball game and we must realize that our armed security forces cannot be everywhere, at all times, to prevent these crimes from happening. It is one thing to sit safely in isolation and decide that guns are still not necessary but it is a completely different case if one of your own family is killed in such a horrific incident. It is often said that if our government outlaws the owning of guns then only the outlaws will have guns. In the present turbulent times this idiom can be amended to include the words "and terrorists" will have guns. Since the Islamic jihad has hit our shores the sale of fire arms, to American citizens, has spiked by fifteen percent. It is currently estimated that fire arms ownership will peak at around three hundred million which is not too much short of a gun for every human being in the USA. If we have to fight, to protect ourselves, then we will be prepared to face any who are determined to hurt us. We understand that they are too cowardly to announce where or when this will happen but they had better pray to Allah because they are likely to meet him sooner than intended. We must now realize that we are living in a nightmare and that the doves must now learn to fly with the hawks or become a casualty of this barbaric and vicious enemy. I only hope that we can get through these trying times and emerge triumphant at the other side. If our leaders do not rise to meet this ominous challenge then we must do so ourselves rather than live in fear. The sooner that we get armed and prepared to face this enemy, on their terms, the safer we will be. I still don't own a gun but I can empathize with those people who now find it necessary to do so.

Let me also state, at this stage, that we must not let the sins of a few fall on the many good and honest Islamic American people. We must concentrate on the evil minority, of this religious sect, that have a murderous and maniacal mind set. To attack the regular law abiding members of this religion would only disenchant more of them to turn against us and exasperate the situation even more. Right now we only have a regional war coupled with some random foreign attacks and this is what we must concentrate on at the present. If we make it a total world wide religious conflict this could possibly escalate into to an apocalyptic situation and neither side will ever benefit from that.

There is another aspect to this perplexing subject, of gun ownership, which is directed at who should or should not be allowed buy them. Pro-gun choice advocates say that it is not guns that kill people, it is people who kill people. By this they mean that tighter control should be put on who should legally be allowed to purchase fire arms. Many murders, by guns, have been committed by mentally disturbed or deranged people. For instance the man who shot and killed John Lennon had a long history of mental illness but was still allowed to legally walk into a gun dealership and purchase a gun with hollow point bullets. Any person with a diminished mental capacity should be in an official computer data bank so that all gun dealers can double check any person to see if they should, in all good concience, be sold a fire arm. If such a person then goes out and buys an illegal gun, on the street, then the seller of that weapon should also be arrested, for aiding and abetting a crime, especially if that gun is later used in a murder. At gun shows the legal gun dealer is fine but the private gun trader, an unofficial type of gun seller, should also have to become legally certified. This will close off yet another avenue where criminals can purchase fire arms, to commit crimes, which sometimes turn into deadly affairs. There is no panacea to stop this curse but crime could be minimized with tighter gun control. Outlaws and mentally unstable people will eventually be listed and punished for their misdeeds whether accidental or done with malice of fore thought.

CHAPTER SEVENTEEN
Never Say Die

For a slightly built guy I have endured a great deal of hurt in my time so much so that it has recently dawned on me that I have developed a high tolerance of pain. Before I was eleven years old I had my troublesome tonsils and appendix surgically removed and had a load of minor afflictions to boot. At age of eight a neighborhood kid shot me in the leg with a blunted arrow from a real sized long bow which he had been given for Christmas. Although the tip was blunted, for shooting in target practice, it still left a permanent indentation on the calf of my left leg. I fell from a substantially high tree which left me winded on the ground, for about five minutes, before I could raise enough strength to stand up again. I also jumped off the roof of a school single story building knocking my teeth through my lower lip. It wasn't the height that caused this injury it was the concrete path, which I had miscalculated the width of, at my point of take off. I had not jumped from the point at which I sized up my daring do. Half way down I realized my miscalculation but by then it was too late and I had to be carried home bleeding profusely. Add to the permanent scar, on my lower lip, I had sport related injuries such as black eyes, cuts and bruises which is why my mother's hair turned prematurely gray.

At the age of eleven I was enrolled for the school where I would be educated up to the age of sixteen. Here, instead of playing with my local pals, I was thrown into a mixture of boys from a distance of twenty miles from around my town and neighborhood. Some of these boys were from mining towns and farming communities and although they were my age some of them were much bigger and harder. Playing rugby with some of these boys was a real eye opener and their vicious crash tackles left me breathless. Because of these bigger boys, during that period in time, I was always limping, aching or carrying some sort of pain. The code back then was that you never showed your pain, no matter how bad, and therefore you were considered to be a man of good standing. Anyone who was heard crying or complaining, about his particular injuries, was considered a wimp and thus cast out by this harder group of boys. I adopted this silent code and, although being one of the smallest boys of my age, I was accepted as now being a tough little guy. At fifteen, being now tough, scrappy and fast, I played rugby for my school team weighing in at a low of one hundred and twenty pounds. I was taught, by some valley boys, how to tackle ferociously and bring down just about anything that moved.

With this never say die attitude I was noticed, by a local team scout, and consequently at the age of sixteen I left school and began to play in a men's league with honorable distinction. The toughness level was ratcheted up quite a bit as I was now competing against hardened coal miners and steel workers. On a Christmas Eve I broke my left collar bone playing, in a Cup game, against a team of big steel mill workers, from Ebbw Vale, on a dreary day. This happened around 3 PM and I had to catch a public transport bus to a hospital, five miles south, and back to my home which was now a further ten miles north all while in total agony. I finally arrived home at mid night, took three quick shots of whisky and promptly passed out. I had to wear a shoulder brace for three months and was unable to play any sports. A year later, at nineteen years of age, I moved on up north and entered first class rugby up in Cheshire, England where I played until I left to go to America at the age of thirty six. During those years I dislocated both shoulders, broke my right ankle and my lower jaw, which was split completely in half. I also estimate that I had somewhere around a hundred stitches sewn into various facial and head wounds. By now I was a sadist and enjoyed these arduous and frantic times. I thrived on being accepted and respected as someone who could be relied upon when the going got tough. I still have friends from each of these phases, of my sporting life, and it is rewarding to think that I have made such a vivid impression on so many people.

The whole point of relating these events is to highlight the fact that I seem to have developed this high tolerance for pain. When other people around me rant and writhe in agony, from their injuries, I just take my knocks without uttering a single word of complaint. After coming to America I hooked up with a great bunch of guys and played league soccer, up in Michigan, at top amateur level. I was so hardened, by all my rugby knocks, that I never had any major injuries but I did inflict quite a few on my opponents. If ever I found myself in a position where I was about to collide, with an opponent, I would drop my shoulder into his chest. He would go flying into the air then land unceremoniously on the ground, moaning and groaning, while I just stand over him silently grinning. I developed quite a reputation for being tough and because of this a good number of the opposing teams, that I played against, would approach me to join them. I only played where my heart was and that was with my good friends. I played with Dearborn Rovers, Ferndale Internationals and Canton Celtics because I knew most of the players there even before I joined them. I came to Florida in 1999 and played pickup soccer for two years before deciding to hang up my boots, at the tender age of sixty two, having played competitive sports for fifty two consecutive years.

Roughly five years after retiring from all sport activities I was coaxed out of retirement to play soccer again by a guy, from St. Louis, who was now living on the same Florida island as me. It wasn't the actual playing that was hard but the following days when rigor mortise set into my legs which happened consistently for the first two months or so. After my legs finally became used to being exercised again I was literally off and running. I now found myself playing with and against young men who, in many cases, could be my grandsons. Quite often, while playing, I would be kicked or run into by some younger guy but to his astonishment I never once complained or verbally responded, in any way, against this. It became quite common for me to be the topic of conversation, at the bar after the games, for some heroic deed on the field of play. I have met head to head, on the field of play, with some of the toughest young guys and never once have I backed down from any tough situation. Before one game, in an accident in my yard at home, I had ripped the toe nail almost completely off my left big toe. I caused a big sensation when some of the other players saw me taping the nail back into its proper position so that I would be able to play in the upcoming game. It wouldn't have been so bad if it wasn't for the fact that I am predominantly a left footer and would be mainly kicking with that damaged toe. At another time I turned up for a game having just had fifteen stitches sewn into my face under my right eye. I had a piece of cancerous skin removed, that very afternoon, and the doctor gave me explicit instruction not to play. However, when I found out that my team was short of players there was no doubt as to what I needed to do. On another occasion I was carrying a recently dislocated shoulder and no-one expected me to even show up at the field. To their amazement, I showed up with a heavily padded shirt, which I had rigged up at home, from a ladies sanitary product. I was in a great amount of discomfort while playing but somehow I managed to get through the game which, incidentally, we ended up winning. Now that's dedication!

At my highly advanced age I am still able to score the occasional goal or two and when I do it is always celebrated with rousing cheers from the watching crowd. The younger people are amazed that I can still find the net and they even ask for advise to improve their scoring technique. Since my age has made me lose muscle strength in my legs I have adopted the toe shot, ala Ronaldo. If this shot is done perfectly the ball travels at a high rate of speed and is as true as a laser beam. However, if you are just half an inch off dead center, when you strike the ball, it will arc away and sometimes miss the intended target I am probably successful in around a third of these shots but when they do find the net, they are spectacular goals. It is that which makes the spectators ecstatically happy and chants of "The toe, the toe" can be heard rising from the excited spectators. My other ploy, to beat the goal keeper, is as he rushes out to cut down my shooting angle , I just gently lob the ball over his head and into the net. Voila!

It is nice, to say the least, when I am respected by my peers and even more so when most of them are around fifty years younger than I am. The other day I bumped into one of my soccer buddies who was having lunch with another guy. He said to his friend "This is Lyn Clarke, one of the toughest guys you could ever wish to meet." This sincere and unprompted testimony was a shock to me but it enforced the respect that these younger men hold for me. I frequently hear one or other of them say that if they can do what I can do, at my age, they will have fulfilled their life long ambition. In the eleven seasons that I have been playing soccer, on this island, I have only missed four games and that was this past summer when I went back, to the old country, for a family wedding. Although I am comparatively old, the team captains will pick me because they know that they can rely on me. If I say that I will be standing on my head in the middle of Piccadilly Circus, London next Tuesday at 8 PM, I will be there. Even if I am injured or feeling unwell I will still be there because I was taught, at an early age, that if you promise to do something, you bloody well better had. It is called total dedication.

Toughness, unlike skill and technique, is something that you can only learn from long, arduous and continued experiences. You cannot instill it into people who have not earned it the hard way. I have seen large men cry, bleed and even fold under the pressure of severe opposition. Today, in particular, it is difficult to find this quality because kids are given so much without breaking a sweat to earn it. In my day we had to work, from around the age of twelve, for anything we wanted. A lot of the times, even after working hard, we still did not achieve our goals but this, in itself, built character. I was raised and exposed to a hard society run by hard people during hard times. Nothing came easy and anything worth having was worth fighting tooth and nail to get. Incidentally, my father died, when I was three years of age, so I had no parachute to save me when I failed. This at first was a sad loss to me but as I grew older I realized that if I wanted to be somebody, in life, I had better get off my arse and get it done. If I screwed up during some flights of fantasy, that would have been profitable for me, I just had to buckle back down and come up with an alternative way of making up that money. I had numerous set backs, both in sport and business but my inbred determination never wavered and I ploughed on regardless. I was raised at the university of hard knocks and have never regretted my severe upbringing. I became molded into one hard and determined character and eventually failure was not an option. In the final analysis you inevitably are what you make of yourself. Yes, this process can be a frustrating and difficult process but the things that one will learn, on that journey, pays off in later life. This work is well worth the hard earned rewards and any person who tries to cut corners, is somewhat of a fool and is destined to languish in the doldrums of failure for an eternity. Where toughness is concerned there is no substitute for experience and this alone can mold a man of steel.

CHAPTER EIGHTEEN

Skeletons From My Closet

My full and true name is Lyndhurst Rufus Herbert-Clarke. It is rare that I release this information but in keeping with the title of this book, I feel it only right and proper to do so. Yes, this prolonged title has caused me some consternation in the past and some of my boyhood friends still, to this very date, use this as a method of deflating my soaring ego. I am named Lyndhurst after my father who was killed in WWII when I was a three year old child. He was named so from a town, in the New Forest, where his parents honeymooned and, I assume, where he was conceived. The name Rufus came from my father's distinguished father who was a well heeled bar owner and sportsman who was also known as a race horse owner. The double surname of Herbert- Clarke came from the last name of both my parents and the Herbert was added at the insistence of my mother. It is a well known fact the my father's mother did not want him to marry my mother but my determined father was resolute and would not bend to her request. The reason for her objection was that my mother's family were poor working class people who lived in a council owned home. My mother's father, Herbert Herbert, yes you read it right, and my father's father, Rufus Clarke, had both passed away before the marriage and although my father's mother was on the wedding photograph she looked obviously unhappy.

This situation meant that the relationship with my grand mother, on my father's side, towards our side of the family was strained to say the least. After my father died, when his boat blew up while he was serving in the Royal Navy, we were occasionally invited to visit her but the atmosphere was always some what frigid and the conversation at a minimum. The only reason why we were invited at all was for her to see my sister Ann and me, and so my mother was more like an onlooker. My father's brother Geoff always lived with Grandma Clarke but he was very subservient to her every whim and although I liked him, he was not the man that my father was. In fact he had wanted to marry one particular girl but not having the tenacity to fight when his mother forbid it he capitulated to her edict. He made a huge mistake as it was to shape the rest of his life as he remained a bachelor and lived with his mother until the day she eventually died. My father was a well known rugby player, in our area, and so was made of sterner stuff but poor old Uncle Geoff was not so strong willed and could not say "Boo" to a goose. He was his mother's whipping boy for most of his life. He was kind and friendly and never learned to drive a car and so he would spend hours roaming the local hills and was greeted and recognized by just about everyone he met along the way. When I was a young boy he would take me on his meandering walks and I was amazed by just how many people stopped and talked with him. He was a sad character and it was my early impression that the people who acknowledged him, along the way, felt a certain degree of empathy with his situation. His wandering stopped when he lost one of his legs, to gangrene , and this severely affected his moral. He passed away in what, days gone by, would have described as a pauper's hospital. For around the last twenty years of his life, after his mother's death, he lived completely alone until he, in turn, passed away a sad and lonely man. He did not realize his ambition of marrying the woman he adored but he never met a stranger.

After my father's death my mother was invited to bring us two kids with her to stay with my father's sister Rene who lived in the beautiful town of St. Ives, Cornwall. She was my father's younger and only sister who was married to an attorney who was the Town Clerk of that quaint place. We stayed there for almost the whole year of 1944 and I remember this as a good period of my life. We lived near the waters edge, it was often very sunny and all the neighbors were kind because of our family's circumstances. Now my auntie, because of her husbands exalted position, was highly respected and popular with just about everyone that we met. I don't know about my mother but this made my sister and I feel important and well received by one and all. In spite of our sad situation this proved to be a rather happy period of our childhood days. I remember wading in the sea and searching for crabs in the rocky pools which were left after the tide ebbed. My uncle Bill Rainey-Edwards was a soft spoken man but was always deeply respected for his sage advice. The town's people would stop him, in the street, to ask for some guidance on their current bone of contention. He would be extremely diplomatic when listening to their plaints but would only offer them guidance at his office. For me, as a four year old boy, this was heady stuff and, to this very day, I have a photo of him shaking hands with Princess Anne when, for some reason unknown to me, she visited St. Ives. This was an impressive and somewhat happy period of my young life.

When we returned, to our home town, we were then invited to stay with my mother's Aunt Hester at her and Uncle Tom's large home. At this time we were virtually penniless with our mother trying to bring us two kids up on her own. She was waiting for my father's death benefits to come through from the Ministry of War who distributed the finances that we so desperately needed but they seemed to be in no particular hurry to do so. If it wasn't for the kindness of other family members we would have been out on the streets and probably begging for food. These were tough and meager times which could only be understood by someone who had lived through such demanding days. The government did eventually give us food stamps which we, in turn, gave to Aunt Hester to supply all of us with food and to repay our hosts for their kindness. She was an extremely introverted person and only spoke, at all, if someone asked her a direct question. Uncle Tom, who was a carpenter at a local coal mine, was always doing house repairs or improvements. He also planted loads of vegetables and a selection of fruits which could survive that damp climate. He would pick and bring them into the kitchen where Aunt Hester would clean , dice and cook them. We lived very much off the land and with the food stamps, to get other essentials, we were able to survive those meager, harsh and desperate times. Because of this strenuous upbringing, and the fact that our small portions of food did not stretch out my stomach, my body is lean and mean to this very day. I survived all this and remain healthy and it grieves me, somewhat, when I see that many of today's children are over weight. This indicates that their food intake is way more than their body requires for normal activities. This aspect, plus the introduction of computers, is producing a whole generation of youngsters with unhealthy bodies and idle minds.

Finally my mother received the death benefits that she so desperately needed and, although it did not compensate for the loss of a loved one, it was enough for her to put a down payment on a modest house. We moved in with very little furniture but we were safe, dry and fed. Seven years after my father's death and a good deal of additional trauma, my mother met and married a man who had just been demobilized from his duties in the Army. He had been a slight acquaintance of my mother and father, from before the War, and after a whirlwind romance they were wed and he moved into our home which was quite a shock for my sister and me. With his war pension, several years later, we moved down off the hillside into a small store which my mother and he bought together. Before their re-acquaintance my mother had already taken a weekend job as a nurse at a nearby hospital. Her three nights of work brought in additional money and for the first time in my life, at the age of ten, we were enjoying relative comfort. The reason that I have related these facts is to show that even in the worse of times people can produce astounding results. At that tender age I vowed that I would never be poor again no matter what I legally had to do. I have worked long, hard and continuously and I advise young ambitious people to adopt the same work ethic because no matter how lowly the job is, if they work hard and conscientiously they will always be recognized as a person of note.

My Auntie Rene, just like her two brothers, was educated at a private school and thus was brought up with a haughty attitude. Uncle Bill took positions, latterly, as the Town Clerk of Ipswich, in East Anglia, and finally Bridgewater, in the county of Somerset. Obviously he and Auntie Rene lived a much classier existence than our side of the family and the old animosities prevailed. When Uncle Bill passed away Auntie Rene moved back to our home town, just two miles from us, but we still only saw her occasionally. Because my mother had remarried a working class man, whose family was thought to be of low standing, my aunt's wealthy upbringing would not allow her to mix with us on a regular basis. She occasionally visited, mainly to see my sister and me, but her attitude towards my mother was very condescending. She eventually passed away but, even in death, she snub my mother by cutting her out of her will. She left some monies for my sister and I but never gave my mother one red cent. She left her house and all her possessions to an old female school chum, who she had reacquainted with, during her few years of return home. This was her final act of contempt towards my mother who raised her niece and nephew with very little help from a family who could well afford to do so. Aunty Rene lived on a high plateau of moral ground but on occasions it must have been extremely cold up there. Her snobbish up bringing and indignation meant that by staying aloof she missed out on so many simple but happy family times. It would have cost nothing for her to reach down and extend the hand of friendship to my mother but her frosty demeanor kept her in a permanent state of frozen animation. That is the sad saga of two sides of an inter-married family, who were divided by differing social levels. If my father had not been killed, he would have been head of the family and would have stamped out this pathetic situation. He would have stood steadfastly by my mother's side and would not have tolerated a family split. From what I have learned, about my father, he was a no nonsense kind of guy and would have squashed any hint of resentment towards my mother and her side of the family. Our lives would have contained a great deal of happiness and we would have had a vastly improved existence.

CHAPTER NINETEEN
Sea Mist On The Horizon

There is a huge conflict brewing down in the Caribbean Sea region. The country of Columbia has just released news that its navy has now independently located the wreck of a long lost Spanish galleon named the San Jose. Why is this report, of yet another ship wreck, causing such great turmoil? Because aboard this galleon is the highest value of salvageable wealth ever anticipated. In fact the amount of wealth, when realized, is so massive that it will rocket this otherwise relatively poor country into being debt free for many years to come. It is estimated that the combined collection, of gold, silver and emeralds, could be valued at around seventeen billion, yes that's with a "B", dollars at today's rate of currency. This is somewhat resembling a similar case of when the now famous Florida salvage man Mel Fisher found the Atocha. At that point, in time, it was the most valuable Spanish galleon find in recorded history but the San Jose is going to make that treasure look like chicken feed. Fisher was paid handsomely for his arduous, timeless work, on that project, but it did not compensate him for the tragic loss of his son who was killed in an under water salvaging accident. I have been to Fisher's museum in Key West, where a portion of his magnificent finds are on display, and my wife Sharon is now wearing one of the smaller silver coins, from that find, on a chain around her neck. All the security, that this museum had, could not stop some scalawag from stealing a solid gold bar from a plate glass display case.

Now you would think that such an historic discovery would be happily met with congratulations all around. However, this is not the case as an American based company named Sea Search Armada has stepped forward to announce that it was they, in fact, that told the Columbian government the vicinity of where the San Jose was located back on March 4th, in 1982. They also point out that in 2007 the Columbian supreme court issued a proclamation that S S A was rightful in their claim of finding the San Jose's wreck and should thus be allotted fifty percent of the wealth there in. This has opened up a whole new can of worms as this, without a doubt, proves that the S S A company is the initial discoverer of this vast wealth. The amount of wealth on this wreck could equal the gross national product of more than half the countries existing on this planet today. I anticipate that to settle this dispute, in the not too distant future, this set of circumstances will bring about a protracted and highly contended legal debate to settle this dispute. This will be one of the most fascinating law cases to come before a judge for many years and it will be avidly followed by hundreds of interested people from around the world. I say this because not only is Columbia and the S S A company in competition but Spain has also made a claim for this treasure, of unimaginable wealth, because it was in their possession when lost around three hundred years ago. Others say that since all the silver was taken from the Potosi mines in Bolivia and the gold from Peru that these countries might also have a claim to part of these riches. This is so intriguing that I can envisage a new and exciting Pirates of the Caribbean/ Indiana Jones type movie bubbling on the horizon.

A mysterious individual, who the Columbian government claims gave them a new earlier location for the San Jose, has been described as an Ernest Hemmingway look alike who approached them at an Embassy reception. This makes him somewhat tall, bearded and Caucasian which doesn't give too many leads to be identity. He also told them that he had been studying ship wrecks for thirty eight years and his information was highly probable. It is claimed that he presented the Columbian government with slightly different co-ordinates, than those previously provided by S S A, from a hitherto unknown map which he found during his investigations. Now if you think about it, this map could only come from either a Spanish sailor, who survived this encounter, or alternatively from the records of the British war ship which sank her. It was common practice, back in those days, that all international sea going vessels had to keep precise daily records of their travels. The captain would log every significant detail of each day's activities and an event, of this magnitude, would be note worthy. I have to assume that if the British ship's crew would have known about the vast wealth, on the San Jose, they would have forcefully boarded her and not sunk her. It is also my view that in the mayhem, of a fierce battle, it is unlikely that someone would have had the fore thought to retrieved the ship's log as it was sinking. I could be wrong but I favor the fact that the location of the San Jose would more likely have come from the log of the victorious British ship. The British are well known as being hoarders, when it comes to records keeping, in which case the location map details would probably have been found in the Royal Naval Academy archives at Chatham, London. Perhaps the white bearded foreigner, or Hemmingway look alike, is possibly an ex-British naval officer who had special access to this type of classified information. Of course this is all supposition on my part and until the Columbian government reveals his true identity this shrouded mystery will endure.

So where does all this lead to? Both parties, the S S A and Columbia, have similar yet slightly different co-ordinates for the San Jose's location. The Columbian government says that they previously did a deep water investigative search but there was nothing found at the co-ordinates presented to them by S S A. In their defence S S A has said that the Columbian government moved the goal posts, before investigating the co-ordinates that they had provided, in a back door attempt to try and deny them of their share of the spoils. They also added that either there are two galleons near to each other, which is extremely unlikely, or they have found the same one a second time. The slight difference in co-ordinates, between the two vying parties, comes about in a unusual manner. There are two important factors that must be considered for the exact location of the San Jose's location. One is the prevailing wind patterns on the day of the sinking and the other, obviously, is the precise co-ordinates. Why the S S A and Columbia has different information, to identify the co-ordinates, is because back in the 1980's there was a margin of error deliberately allowed and so, to keep the exact location a closely guarded, secret S S A stated "Can be found in the immediate vicinity of." S S A states that this margin of error was not taken into consideration when the details were incorporated by Columbian's law system. Here lies the bone of contention, between the two parties, thus this might have to be settled by a non partisan, independent international tribunal. No matter which way the ball bounces one or the other, of these two entities, is in for an enormous amount of incremental wealth. The mysterious foreign Hemmingway character, if still alive, will no doubt be at the center of this earth shattering dispute. The Columbian government has always said that this person gave them his findings because he was only interested in the history, archeology and cultural aspects of the San Jose's demise. He has also been quoted as saying that the cargo and treasures of the sunken ship, when finally recovered, should be placed in a public museum for all to see. Wow, a benevolent James Bond type is hard to find in these mercenary days of self serving individuals. However, as they say concerning all unsolved mysteries, stay tuned for further installments on this most fascinating turn of events.

Incidentally, as a foot note, Mel Fisher is still salvaging, in the waters surrounding the Dry Tortuga Islands off Key West, Florida. Here, he has discovered a second wrecked galleon which was sunk by the same storm that took down the Atocha. This ship, the Santa Maria, was part of yet another attempt of Spain to transport treasures, taken from the Incas, back to their country. Eventually the Spanish explorers were guilty of wiping out that whole native South American civilization. Only the Incan ruins, such as Machu Picchu, still remains to bear witness of them ever having existed at all. Spain, in the name of the catholic church, robbed them and left disease and devastation in return. I have recently heard that the Spanish government has now graciously dropped their claim for part of the San Jose's wealth. Let's face it, their claim was fraudulent as the wealth was stolen goods by anyone's standard. Perhaps their national concience has finally kicked in.

Incidentally, while on this subject of unimaginable wealth, figures have just recently been released which state that the sixty two richest people of the world have the combined equal wealth to half of the worlds human population. Another comparison also states that these fortunate people have more wealth than the combined national products of forty two of the world's lesser developed countries. Add to this the stunning statistic the fact that four hundred and ninety two of the world's current billionaires reside and operate in the good old USA. These mind boggling statistics shows, with clarity, the extreme difference between the absolute rich and the extreme poor. No wonder so many impoverished people are abandoning their ruined countries and, with the dream of immigrant status, they are flooding into richer nations in the hope of a better life style. Alas, it is said that drowning people always take down those nearest to them and so I hope that these desperate beings will not bankrupt their generous host countries in a frantic attempt to improve themselves. They might just have to curb their enthusiasm, for instant success, and copy those who have gone before them and toil endlessly to achieve their dream of a good standard of living.

CHAPTER TWENTY

Unexpected Guests

It has recently been estimated that there are somewhere in the region of thirteen million illegal immigrants currently living in the U S A. In the past sixteen years, that I have lived in Florida, the rate of illegal entries has more than doubled. These illegal people costs the American tax payers a whopping one hundred and thirty three billion dollars per year. This is what their taxes would contribute to our country if they were legally paying their share. They want to live here permanently and avail themselves to all of our amenities but not pay anything for them. Because these illegal aliens are mainly from Mexico and Central American countries, they are almost entirely of the catholic faith and do not believe in birth control. It doesn't take an Einstein to figure out that, if their rapid growth of population continues unchecked, it will not take too long for them to be the majority of our society. If they conceive a baby here it automatically becomes an American citizen and that child's parents, now, cannot be deported under current law.

Once an alien family becomes secretly established they then send for the rest of their extended family to get here, as quick as they can, anyway they can. Therefore the immigrant population is increasing by leaps and bounds.

This cycle of invasion, by foreigners, is being repeated all over America and is a hugh stress on an already over strained economy. Many of them have multiple aliases and if found out, in any given State, they just move to another one and change their names. Because they have no legal paperwork they cannot apply for a drivers license and so they buy a car privately and then drive anyway without insurance. This deception mainly accounts for the numerous amount of hit and run vehical incidents. If they work at all it is always for another person, from their country of origin, who pays them cash to avoid a paper trail which could lead to them being found. If they, or any member of their family, needs medical attention they cannot be refused treatment but by giving false names and addresses they are never found and therefore all their hospital bills go unpaid. On the rare occasions where one of them is found out they are deported back to their country of origin, at our country's cost, but within a short space of time they get back here again. I had a friend who was a supervisor on a commercial building site where the law would swoop in unannounced and round up a gang of illegal workers. They were then sent back to their home country but around two weeks later they would be back at his office door requesting their jobs back. They will take these jobs because although they are paid less, than a regular citizen, it is still considerably more than they would be paid at home. The illegal workers will also live on as little as possible so that they can send the majority of their ill gotten gains back to support family members still living in their country of origin.

When illegal aliens slip through the net they tend to reside around other people with the same problem of not wanting to be found. They congregate in specific small enclaves, in any given town, which over time evolve into barrios. These conclaves, within a town, are populated by this foreign class of people who are very secretive and protective of each other. These areas, after a while, become unruly and are the centers for all sorts of illicit business transactions and become dangerous for anyone, outside of them, to even enter. They become ruled by street drug gangs and the violent crime rates there rise astronomically. This has been a predominately American problem for more than fifty years but it has now reach a level of unmanageable proportions. Dishonest smugglers are making fortunes with payments from illegal aliens to get them across the southern borders of California, New Mexico, Arizona and Texas. Often these foreigners, to pay for their passage across, will smuggle cocain and marijuana into the U S A. This presents even more problems for our border guards and police, to contend with, and all this extra expense is paid for by the legal American citizens. I cannot blame people for wanting a better standard of living but it should not come free of charge or be paid for by other legal citizens. If foreigners want to live in America let them go through the legal channels, as I did, and although this is a long and laborious procedure it is well worth the trouble, in the long run, for the peace of mind and security that it affords.

Because of the wars, in the Middle East region and African countries, this has plunged Europe into the same dire set of circumstances. In the past year it is estimated that one million illegal immigrants have fled their home lands and poured into Europe. All these bedraggled people expect to be clothed, fed, housed and given medical treatment all at someone elses expense. Around eighty percent of these illegal immigrants are single men, between about eighteen and thirty years of age, which begs the question why they are not back, at home, fighting against the terrorists who are destroying their lands. They come across the Meditaranian Sea, by boats, and land in either Greece, if from the East, or Italy if from Africa. However this is usually not their final goal of destination as they desire to go to the more benevolent countries like Germany, Sweden or Britain. They have already been taught that these are the countries where they can receive the most abundance of social wellfare.

They have no desire to live in such countries like Poland, Bulgaria, Slovenia, Hungary or even Greece, where they disembarked, because they are aware of the financial restrictions there. The majority of these particular illegal foreigners are of the Islamic faith which means that they are bringing with them a whole different life style and expect the mainly non Islamic citizens to accept and tolerate their customs. If some of these young men do not find jobs, in their newly adopted countries, they eventually become disgruntal and are prone to commit acts of terrorism against the host countries that accepted them. This is akin to biting the hand that has fed them which is totally unacceptable.

Currently, in America, we have a Republican candidate who is running to be nominated for the exalted position as the President of the USA. He has promised that, if he is elected, he will build a wall across the entire length of the Mexican border to stop this access from the south. He has also said that he will make the country of Mexico pay for its construction. This sounds rather drastic but how else can we stop illegal aliens from just walking into our land? He has also said that until the current government can come up with a precise plan, to combat terrorists entering from the Middle East, that we should ban everyone from that region from coming to our country. This again sounds drastic but to stop people who mean to harm us, at the expense of upsetting a few who are harmless, seems a good deal to me. Remember, in WWII all Japanese emigrants were rounded up and put into internment camps to ensure our safety. Political correctness, the scourge of our society, has previously discouraged anyone from stating such drastic measures but it is what the majority of Americans have silently wanted for years past. Our elected politicians have almost , to a man, succumbed to this assumed required political correctness strategy and it has made them virtually impotent of being able to think logically. The enemies of the USA have been quick to recognize this political weakness, which has misguidedly been forced upon us, as the weak chink in our armor and has used this to their advantage. The current President of America has adopted a wait and see tactic when what is needed is a decisive leader who is pro-active in matters that concern our home land security. This present course of continual inactivity is recognized, and taken advantage of, by our enemies as their opportunity to prey upon us. The next President will have to be much stronger on his/her decision, to protect the American people, wherever they live around the world. The current President wanted a legacy of being the one that brought peace to our nation. However, his decision to withdrawl our troops from Afghanistan and Iraq was the catalyst that encouraged the terrorist, in those regions, to become reinvigorated and rise up again. This is the direct result of choosing, for President, a man who had little or no expertise in foreign affairs. His contemrories, from around the world, consider him to be under qualified and therefore they do not respect any of his diplomatic decisions, particularly concerning the Middle East.

I would like to make it abundantly clear that I am not bigoted against any individual nationalities nor classes of people. Because I have had to work continuously, throughout my life, to attain what I now have achieved I expect all others, no matter how lowly their beginning, to do the same. Therefore, I am staunchly against free handouts to people who had the same opportunity as me but chose to take the path of least resistance and rely on others to provide for them. In other words they want all the trappings of a affluent life but expect those comforts to be provided to them by others who are gainfully employed. I remember hearing a story of a person who, after leaving school at sixteen, turned up two years later, on Graduation Day, insisting to be allowed entrance. On being refused, by the school staff, a huge unsightly scene ensued which dampened the proceedings for those students who had worked so hard and diligently to complete their schooling. This single under achieving person, by instigating this shameful display had unwittingly, or perhaps intentionally, detracted from the enjoyment of all the other legitimate graduates. This is typical of the concept, that some lazy people have, of doing as little as possible but expecting everything. My opinion is extended to these types of people, from around the world, who think that they are owed something that they did not rightfully work for or deserve. They envy the good life, that others have honestly toiled for, and will take it by any means, legal or not, to gratify their own selfish needs.

People involved in the illegal use or the distribution of drugs are obvious examples of this selfish, do nothing and expect everything, illness. I do not refer to the casual cannabis smoker but to those who rob, steal and pillage to get their daily fix, of cocaine or heroin, without which they cannot survive yet another worthless day. Such spineless people lack any real goals in life and have lost touch with reality. They continually live in a surreal world of phantom desires but lack any semblance of true achievement. In biological terms, such creatures are classified as parasites because they rely on a host body to provide all their needs. They are a blight on any civilized society because they prey on the innocent, just so they can drift off into a state of total oblivion in the hope of attaining their unrealistic desires. They are, in fact, the real walking dead as they stumble through life, trying to resemble genuine people, while living outside the laws of the land. What poor excuses for human beings they have gradually and inevitably become. This summary might seem blind and viciously unkind but I have tried the more sympathetic style of understanding and, I can assure you, it does not work. The people, with this mind set, have absolutely no concept of fair play or being reasonable towards others. They will even sink as low as to steal from their own family and, in their own minds, justify the actions of this flagrant disloyalty. They will even let their own young children go without food than them go without their drugs. You can throw the rule book out of the window because nothing is sacred with this dysfunctional gene puddle.

CHAPTER TWENTY-ONE
The Disintegration Of Nature

There is a troubling trend which has recently come to light although it has existed , to a minor degree, for a good number of years gone by. I am referring to the dire circumstance that is now adversely affecting the, all important, domestic honey bee. Some years back bee keepers, from around America, noticed a mysterious massive down trend in the bee population. When these increased reports, of this unusual occurrence, reached the Environmental Protection Agency alarm bells began to ring. The investigators were sent out, throughout the land, to try and find out what on earth was causing such a apocalyptic turn of events. After prolonged and intense studies they came up with a united agreement that it was we humans that had, unwittingly, become the culprit of this plight. Farmers involved in grain, vegetable or fruit farming, had been spraying their crops with a pesticide not knowing that it contained a chemical that adversely affected the honey bees. The pesticide is extensively used by anyone growing oranges, grape fruit, blackberries, cherries, apples, avocados, cucumbers, onions, cantaloupes, cranberries, pumpkin and sun flowers. So as you can see we are not talking about a small problem but one that will affect virtually every family in the country. The honey bees pollinate all of these crops and so if they disappeared these crops would suffer and perhaps disappear from the face of the earth.

I will not name the manufacturer of this particular pesticide but it is available on public records. The chemical that is causing this massive problem has a nicotine imitating property which is specifically named Imidacloprid and can be found in one hundred and eighty eight farm products. The honey bee comes in contact with this when pollinating, any of the afore said crops, and ultimately takes it back to its hive and infects the rest of the bees at that location. With so many honey bees providing their valuable service, it means that literally millions and millions of them have been infected and, in most cases, have died. These tiny creatures, which we casually take for granted, are extremely necessary to our well being that if they were to disappear our lives can be adversely affected forever. In California alone, in 2011, one hundred tons of this chemical was applied during farming operations there. The E P A is now frantically researching and observing the affects of any farm product containing this substance but so far nineteen percent of samples taken have far exceeded the allowed level of contamination. The E P A is to continue a full assessment of all risks, posed by the troublesome chemical, by the end of 2016 after which time they will tighten the control, over these pesticides and the manufacturer of them. This first test will be done in co-operation with the State of California and Canada. This will be followed by three more examinations, of Neon-Icotinoids in farm products, to be done in specific locations around the USA. Honey bees are used to polinate crucial food crops and contribute to bringing in around $14 billion in value to the agricultural economy nation wide. In studies, of them, it has been found that high levels of this particular group of chemicals decrease foraging, failure of queen bees, breakdown of hive communications and causes colony behavioral confusion. All this, brought on by intense commercial management in the farm industry, has been blamed for the epic collapse that began a decade ago. Now that we are monitoring this problem the full scale col-lapse of colonies has abated, over the past few years, but the bee mortality rate remains abnormally high. I previously touched on this subject in one of my earlier books but back then no-one knew exactly what was causing this problem. Now, that they have a better handle on it, let us hope that we have caught this popula-tion lowering trend in time and that we can restore nature's bal-ance back to its normal condition.

There is also another slightly distressing nature problem which, from time to time, pops up along our local Gulf of Mex-ico beach waters on Florida's western coast. It is locally dubbed Red Tide and mainly appears at the peak of summer, in the shallower waters, when the ocean temperature is at its hottest. The proper name for this phenomina is Karenia Brevis and is the result of an unusual growth of plangton, or an algae bloom, which occasionally plagues the county of Manatee where I re-side. It has also been reported in other Florida Gulf side coun-ties such as Pinellas, Hillsborough, to the north of us, and Sara-sota, Lee, Collier and Charlotte to the south. In shallow waters, where the plankton is nearer to the surface, it can thrive but it dissipates in the vastness of deeper waters. The affect, of this intrusive visitor, is that the increased algae sucks the oxygen out of the water which in turn suffocates the fish. This only af-fects the smaller fish, who tend to linger in the shallows, where as the bigger fish are unaffected in the deeper waters. Unfortu-nately, it also adversely affects the manatee population, which lingers in the shallows, and kills around 150 to 300 of them each time it appears. This ill fated event usually begins around October/November, when the constant sunshine throughout the summer caused the ocean to reach its maximum tempera-ture, and then lasts into February/March when the waters cool again. During this period of time many dead fish are washed up along our entire beach fronts and even in the inter-coastal water ways. This is significantly heralded by the mass gath-ering of turkey vultures which can be observed circling over head. People who have respiratory problems also experience some breathing discomfort but it is a temporary condition. Our local and internationally known ocean laboratory Mote Marina, located on the neighboring island of Long Boat Key, is at the fore front of investigating this puzzling phenomenon. Once again I have briefly eluded to this subject in the past but here again we are much nearer to achieving a possible antidote and hopefully prevent this from reoccurring. I will not be at all surprised if, in the final analysis, it is found that Florida's citrus growing industry is largely to blame. Their use of phosphorous, as a growth enhancer, is probably then washed by our heavy summer rains into the surrounding waters. If this chemical is successful in assisting the growth of crops then, by the same token, it would also assist in the growth of sea plangton which, in turn, deprives the shallows of oxygen. Naturally the fruit industry, because of possible impending legal action and fines which could affect their profits, is denying any such implication. However, I have an inkling that they are in self denial and are ultimately responsible, and therefore guilty, of being directly involved. I wait, with bated breath, for the findings of the investigation by the Florida Fish & Wildlife Commission, so that this irritating issue can finally be put to bed.

While at the ocean, a small but important disagreement has arisen between two sets of local fishermen. This fish tale, between two sea salt factions, has pitted the crabbers and the beach rod fishermen against each other. The crab fishermen lower their pots to the bottom of the sea bed and mark their location with floating buoys. The rod fishermen, particularly at night when shark fishing, take their baited lines out to sea by boat and then come back to shore and wait for a hit. The trouble occurs when they get a large fish on their line and it begins to frantically struggle in the hope of breaking free. As the fish thrashes about and swims in all directions it sometime gets wrapped around a crab pot marker line. The crabbers have accused the rod fishermen of cutting their lines and thus render finding the pot, and the crab catch, virtually impossible. The crabbers also say that at a time when their pots should be full of crabs they are coming up empty and accuse the rod men of stealing their catch. It will not lead to gun fights, as between the cattle ranchers and the sheep farmers of the old west, however the situation is becoming intensely heated. The crabbers are commercial fishermen and rely on their catch to eke out a living, whereas the rod fishermen are predominantly amateur. This has caused quite a stir, in this island community, and the wife of one crabber was recently arrested after assaulting a rod fisherman. A meeting has been arranged by the State Fisheries Authority but the outcome is pending. Nowhere on earth is idyllic, not even here on beautiful Anna Maria Island, as people will always fight others for what they feels is rightfully theirs. Let us hope that civilized heads will prevail and that an amiable agreement will be reached by both parties so that harmony can be restored. This island is too small and the ocean too vast for people to squabble and harbor resentment. As someone who was brought up during Word War II, when the only fish available, to the lower classes, was canned sardines and pilchards, I now love to eat the fresh and succulent array of excellent sea food that the fishermen here provide. However, I do not wish them to kill each other just for the privilege of doing so. It seems that when tempers flair, in situations like this, it provides the capacity to repeat with numbing regularity. This, if you'll excuse the pun, could blow everything out of the water.

In spite of all the age worn platitudes and attitudes, when civility goes there is justice but when justice goes there is war. On a lighter note the only thing that I know of, that can be eaten and yet still told, is a fish tale. For money strapped boat owners, the definition of B O A T simply means "Break out another thousand."

CHAPTER TWENTY-TWO
Unaccounted Wealth

Have you ever wondered why it is that the rich always get richer? Obviously when a person is extravagantly rich the monies that he earns, from interest, out weighs what they can possibly spend and so his money keeps on multiplying. However his wealth is compounded by the taxes that he avoids paying by disguising where the money is kept. Or to use another term, where the money is hidden. A startling revelation has just come to light when previous secret documents have been leaked that makes public a list of all the people, around the world, that have secret stashes of wealth. This massive leek has blown wide open a view into the vast and murky world of shell companies and just how the wealthy conceal their monies.The leak has exposed the trail of dark money, which flows through the global finance system, while stripping national treasuries of massive tax revenues. The data breach occurred at a little known yet powerful Panamanian law firm which has offices in Miami, Las Vegas and a presnce in thirty five other locations around the world. This firm is one of the top five, in the world, that creates shell companies which although can be legitimate, quite often are a smoke screen to dodge taxes and launder monies. The documentation, of all these corporate misdealing, was mysteriously delivered to a German newspaper based in Munich and has created a good deal of attention all over the world. It appears the genie is out of the bottle. The archive states that twelve country and several former world leaders maintain off shore shell companies and several prominent figures close to Vladimir Putin are also named as having funneled as much as two billion dollars through these avenues. Others exposed, by the leak, are the Prime Ministers of Iceland, Malta, Ukraine and Pakistan, a bag man for Syria's President Bashar Assad, a close friend of Mexican President Pena Nieto and family members of Chinese President Xi Jinping. Added to all this is the monarchs of Saudi Arabia and Morocco, some middle eastern royalty, leaders of the top soccer FIFA organization and twenty nine billionaires all listed in Forbes Magazine as being in the top fifty richest people in the world. Also mentioned are sixty one relatives and associates of current country leaders and one hundred and twenty eight other current or former politicians and top public people. A close friend of Putin is reputed to have funneled away as much as two billion dollars through banks and off shore companies.The most extraordinary allegations, in the archives, concern one of Vladimir Putin's long time close friends whose name appears as the owner of various shell companies. In reality he is a cellist with the Saint Petersburg Symphonic Orchestra. It is even indicated that this man also owns five percent of the biggest bank in Russia which is a remarkable achievement for a meagerly paid musician. On one such shell company, registered in Switzerland, where the question was asked, on the application, "do you personally know any politically exposed person? this man answered "No." The fact that he had known the top politician in Russia, for many years, meant that this was a direct lie. Even such felons as drug traffickers and previously condemned company financial fraudsters can be seen as a signatory in some of these documents. The German newspaper shared all the information with the Washington based International Consortium of Investigative Journalism who is now making a thourough investigation into this mountain of information. These recently released documents contain 2.6 terabytes of precise details and will, I am sure, stir up a hornet's nest of activity and condemnation is most certainly to follow. The documents contain 11.5 million e-mails, financial spread sheets, client records, passport and corporate registries were also obtained. Currently there are three hundred and seventy journalists, from seventy eight countries, all pouring over the data and this is the largest world wide collaberation ever undertaken after a leak of this magnitude.

The Panamanian law firm, whose secret details were released, assert that there is absolutely nothing illegal about their business or it's dealings around the world. Not once in forty years of operation have they ever been charged with criminal wrong doings. The law firms founder said, at an interview on Panamanian television, that this whole affair of blaming his company of misdeeds is like blaming an automaker for a car that was used during a bank robbery. The company has never been scrutinized by any law enforcement department of any country. They simply incorpoate companies, in legal tax havens around the world, for individuals who pay them a fee for so doing. Never the less when the documentation is read in detail there will be some glaring instances that deserve further investigation. Four of the most prolific countries from around the world, where such deals are set up, are Panama in central America, the British Virgin Islands in the Caribbean Sea, the Seychelle Islands off the African Coast and Niue, a remote island in the Pacific Ocean. It appears that the officials of these areas pay little or no attention to this type of transactions but greatly benefit from the wind fall injection of monies which come their way. The recently divulged archives contain the names of fourteen thousand people who are listed as middlemen or intermediaries of these shady shell companies. Even in America States such as Delaware, Nevada and Wyoming they register thousands of corporations annually, often without identification of the true owners of them. In some transactions representatives of wealthy foreign countries , who predict that their future food production will not sustain them, are secretly trying to buy up American farm land under illegal third party ownership, once again through shell companies. Some of the billions of dollars, moving through the USA, come from anonymous foreigners who inflate real estate prices, in cities like Miami, when buying properties outright for cash. The FBI currently knows that between six and ten billion dollars, per year, are laundered through such deals. For our own future security we must know the true identity of the people behind these dubious deals which could adversely affect our country's future.

I could be proved wrong, in the long run, but from where I am sitting it appears that Russia is the arch enemy in a good number of these covert occurrences. In 2008 a close friend of President Vladimir Putin owned a private company which somehow had influence over Russia's largest truck manufacturing company named Kazam. This Putin friend somehow later acquired the majority controll of Kazam but needed foreign investment to solidify it's future. The German car maker Daimler, the following year, bought a ten percent share in that company for two hundred and fifty million dollars. The Russian truck making company went from rags to riches in two years and I wonder who all the money ended up with. The off shore company that handled many Russian deals is Sandalwood Continental Ltd., based in the British Virgin Islands. Two of Putin's close friends bought shares, in this virtually unknown company, in an extremely deliberate and covert manner. Now the foxes really are in the chicken coup with their fingers in every deal that goes through that off shore registering company. It vexes me when I think of all the poor people, struggling in the world today, while a privileged few make millions each day just from shuffling documents across a table in the right direction. This is the same as insider trading because they have the fore knowledge, to increase their wealth, without fear of any reprisal and hide their true identity by using the term "bearer shares."

Russia, it seems, has gone from the Communist ideology back to the Tsarian days of massive wealth belonging to a privileged few. It is obvious by the Russian act of invading the Crimea Peninsular that Putin has his own adgenda and does not give a care as to what the rest of the world thinks of him. When he decides to act, on any particular plan, he is cunning and extremely determined. By opening up this mass of documentation, with all their secretive deals, we might get an insight into what Mr. Putin has in mind for our world's future. I only hope this is not akin to opening Pandora's box.

CHAPTER TWENTY-THREE
The Brotherly Bond

I have a good pal, here in Manatee County, who I have met since I resurrected my soccer playing life style. His name, for the purpose of this story, is Hans and obviously he was born and raised in Germany. As a matter of fact he came from East Germany, when it was under the communist rule, then moved to the western region, of that country, when the Berlin Wall was taken down. After his sister met and married an American citizen she moved to the USA and, several years later, she invited Hans to visit her where she resided in the Chicago area. Hans was, and still is, a very good soccer player and was quickly picked up by a Chicago league German team where he took to their successful side like a duck to water. In fact I have played soccer, here in America, for around thirty five years and, without a doubt, he is easily among the top five best players that I have ever had the privilege to play with. He can play up front in attack and score with regularity, he can play in defense and be virtually impossible to get past, or he can play in goal where he is equally at home. In a nut shell, he can do it all with absolute skill and authority. Although he is tall and large framed his first touches, to control the ball, are so delicate that he makes all

145

aspects of this skill seem extremely easy and natural. In attack he has a burst of speed, from a standing start, that leaves most players in the lurch as he glides by with impunity. He also has several strategic evasive moves which, although everyone who has played with him knows and expects, no-one can ever figure them out and is almost always left trailing in his wake. While in his mid-forties and wearing a knee support on each leg he is still a force to be reckoned with.

Hans lives and breaths football, as it is more commonly known world wide, and if he isn't playing it he is watching it, live or on television, coaching it, discussing it or critiquing it. He and I play in the Island Recreation League, for convenience, and we are among around two dozen hard core soccer fanatics that also play pick up games twice a week, year around, during the off season. This hard core bunch of soccer fanatics includes Brits, Germans, Turks, Croasians, Greeks, Kurds and a strong representation of Americans of various foreign decent. However, when it comes to the recreation league we are divided up, throughout the eight competing teams, because if we were to play together, our group of players would most probably take all the honors at every season. When our band of talented players vie against each other, in this league, we play hard and resolute but never hold any animosity towards their brothers. When it comes to partying, after the games, we are the hardest drinkers and usually the last to leave the bar. We are a brotherhood of physically hard and mentally tough like minded players who can be relied upon for help, no matter how demanding the situation is, on or off the field of play. For me this is reminiscent of my twenty five year rugby playing career when my pals, back in the old country, stood or fell as one no matter how hard the going got. They also were a brotherhood of determined men. Hans also has this type of intense sporting mind set and for him, like me, there is no greater male bonding because when the going gets tough, the tough get going!

Well now that I have set the scene, so far as the soccer involvement is concerned, here is the kicker. My good friend Hans is an illegal immigrant. When his older sister invited him to visit her Hans applied and got a ninety day visitors visa. At this time he was introduced to a German soccer club, from that area, and began playing for them as a guest. The officials of that team were so impressed with his skill and ability, as a player, that they encouraged him to stay longer and promised to find him jobs secretly working for their club members. He ended up being trained as a plumber and again within the German community, of that team, he was given plenty of work and thus was able to eke out a living. Prior to all this, his father and mother were already here, in the USA, and after fearing the intervention of the Immigration Department, Hans quickly moved south to join them here in Florida. Once again he had to earn a living, while flying under the radar, and with his plumbing training he was eventually able to get enough work to keep him gainfully employed. Through all his trials and tribulations Hans has never once ask the government of the USA, or the states of Illinois and Florida, for any handouts or help the way. Unlike many foreigners, who cross our southern borders and expect well fare in the form of medical and living assistance, he has managed completely on his own by continuously working hard in every possible situation. When he broke his ankle, in a soccer game, the rest of our brotherhood stepped up and assisted in every way possible, as brothers should. Never was there ever a hint of him wanting other American citizens to pay for his misfortune and if ever the time comes when an armistice is given, to illegal immigrants, he should be top of that list.

When Hans first came to Florida he lived with his father and mother about two miles away from my house. This is when I first met him, around seven years ago, when he tracked down our island soccer gang and quickly became part of our twice weekly pickup games. His mother was now at the onset stage of Alzheimers and, as this became progressively worse, the father suddenly up and sold the house. As soon as the secret sale went through, and he was paid off, the father booked himself a flight and returned to Germany taking all the money with him. This left Hans to feed, bathe and toilet tend to his aging and debilitated mother while still trying to earn a living. This went on for the best part of three years until his mother was so forgetful that he was worried that she would wander off and be lost. He somehow found a Guatemalan woman to baby sit the mother and allow him to do odd jobs and make some money. Eventually because it would be too costly to put his mother in home care here in the USA, Hans contacted his uncle, back in Germany, to fly over and take the mother back where the German government would pay for her upkeep. This was a great relief for him but, in the meantime, the Guatemalan woman was now entrenched and Hans had inadvertently swapped one burden for another. Roughly two years later his mother finally passed away and was buried, where she wanted to be, back in her home town. This chapter of his life was now closed but his new problem gradually worsened as the new lady, in his life, secretly moved in her otherwise unmentioned teenage gangster son. This whole situation finally came to a head when the son, at sixteen, announced he was soon to be a father and actually had two off springs in quick succession. Although this new problem family didn't live with Hans every time he went to work they all descended on his trailer and cleaned out all the edible items from his refridgerator. The woman hardly ever worked and any money she did earn she spent on partying with her so called girl friends. Our brotherhood all advised Hans to get out of that situation and finally, even though he owned the trailer, he packed up and left without looking back. For the following month or so the carping woman constantly phoned him, probably because the rent was due, but he staunchly ignored her continuous lament.

Through all of these hard and trying times Hans always remained up beat and only mentioned these down times, to us soccer pals, when he got melancholy at the end of the evening while having a few too many brewskies. His soccer game was never adversely affected while living under the shadow of this sordid affair. He is now foot loose and care free again and our after game drinks, at Manatee Beach Cafe, are times that I look forward too with great anticipation. When I mention my German friend, to some of my old buddies back in Wales and England, some are a little perturbed because my father was killed in WWII when we were at war with Germany. To begin with Hans is around twenty years younger than me which means that he was born fifteen years after that conflict ended. Secondly my father, while in the Royal Navy, was not killed in action but died in a tragic explosion while his boat was being prepared for a night excursion across the cruel sea. Thirdly, It was Hitler and his pagan Nazi regime, not the German people, who instigated that war and the German civilians suffered greatly as a consequence of that decision. Another German soccer player named Wolfgang, who I played with up in Michigan, once told me that after that earth shattering war and, as a six year old child, he would scavenge for food in the trash bins and often ate maggot laden rotten potatoes to avoid starvation. While doing this, on a daily basis, he would also have to fend off hunger feral cats and rabid dogs who had by now turned back to a wild state. I can't imagine how anyone could be reduced to such a basic level of human existence.

Before closing the subject of soccer I would like to make a categorical statement that in all my years, of playing this sport, my German team mates have always stood out. I would even go one step further and say that I don't believe that I have ever played with a bad one. This probably explains why that country has, to date, won four World Football Cups and have only been superceded by Brazil who have won five. Having observed them, at close quarters, I put this down to their coaching skills and strict discipline because although they play as individuals they never lose sight of the overall team strategy. Other country national team players often get ruffled, during on field heated altercations, but the Germans do not allow this to detract from their calm and calculated game plan and strictly adhere to their objective. On the other hand England, for instance, during the last four World Cup tournaments, have had two of their major star players sent off while allowing the extreme pressure, of playing the game at top level, get to them. It is rare that a team will ever win, in such circumstances, as the remaining ten field players cannot maintain the level of discipline and energy required for them to succeed.

In a previos book I mentioned another soccer playing buddy of mine who is an avid inventor. We call him Two Touch Tony and although he has moved on in life, we still hear from him on occasions. In his career he has been financially successful but more recently has fallen on tougher times. However, he has since resurrected his career and is working on a new method to purify tainted waters to make them drinkable, particularly for third world countries. At the request of Sir Richard Branson, Tony met with him at his private island compound, near St. Thomas in the British Virgin Islands, and discussed his new invention in detail. Not allowing the grass to grow under his feet he has since moved on with his endeavors and is currently living and working in Denmark at the request of one of that country's leading research laboratories. Obviously I am not at liberty, nor would I, go into significant details of his ongoing venture and I merely mention this fact, at all, to give readers an insight into just how diversified our band of brothers really is. No matter how far we travel in the world or how we fare in life, we will always be connected as a like minded bunch of competitors. A person's life can more accurately be measured by the number of close and sincere relationships that he/she has developed. If you only have this, to your credit, your time on this planet has not been completely wasted.

CHAPTER TWENTY-FOUR

Yo~Ho~Ho~And A Bottle Of Rum

A cross the southern bridge from Anna Maria Island, to the main land of Manatee county, is the last working fishing port and processing plant left in the whole of Florida. The village of Cortez, where it is located, is noted throughout the fishing industry, for this fact. The fishing boats can frequently be seen going out for their catches and returning with their loads. On returning, the white rubber booted fishermen and the industrious process workers are a common sight around the local watering holes. After several weeks at sea, and having been paid off for landing a good catch, the fishermen spend their money, as to be expected, like drunken sailors. This is a robust life pattern and these scenes have been re-enacted, as part of the local sea faring tradition that this area has been known for, in years gone by. To be part of this drinking frenzy is both exciting and mind boggling to witness as the bars are packed to capacity. On land, during the lull times while the fishing fleet is out at sea, the village of Cortez returns to it's normal laid back attitude and the bars remain relatively quiet. However, when the fish are not being caught, times can be tough for these sea farers and idle hands, as they say, can make mischief.

During the mid 1960's through to the mid 1980's the small port of Cortez, with all its accesses to the Gulf of Mexico, became a major part of the illegal drug smuggling trade. This was a well known yet unspoken fact to everyone dealing in this vicarious and secret business. With the many charter boats, continuously coming and going, it was natural for some dubious captains to be tempted into this illegal yet profitable trade. These knowledgeable captains knew every back water and tiny bayous in the area and could stealthily slip in and out. They would disguise their boats by covering up any tell tale signs, as to their identity, and in so doing, made it virtually impossible for the authorities to categorically know who they were chasing. If the Coast Guard ever detected them, they would run for cover and be lost in the labyrinth of mangrove channels and overgrown islets. In a case where the Coast Guard did entrap one of these drug smuggling boats, the crew would throw their bales of contraband overboard as they fled. It was more beneficial to lose their profitable load, and live to fight another day, than end up in jail. Inevitably, one by one, they did eventually get caught and serve jail time but by then most of these small boat captains had a sizeable chunk of money put aside for their inevitable retirement on being released. One of the more notorious, of these modern day pirates, was seen driving a brand new Cadillac and the joke, of that time, was that he was a millionaire mullet fisherman. He made no secret of the fact that during his drug running escapades he had brought in ten ship loads, worth an astronomical amount of dollars, to dockage. Another popular local man, who ran for mayor on the island, got arrested after smuggling pot and only his inevitable jail time prevented him from being elected. Such was the fervor, of the local islanders, due to the trickle down of money that would benefit and enhance their daily lives.

My first visit to this region was around 1983/84 and I stayed at the Casa Del Mar on Long Boat Key which is the next island immediately south of here. On two particular days, during our stay, a sea fog drifted inland which blanketed the ocean and brought the visibility down to around just ten yards. On my second day there I was watching the local evening news, on television, when it showed that a quantity of marijuana bales had been found drifting just off shore. It seems that a smuggler was either being vigorously pursued or had lost his bearings for his rendezvous and had jettisoned his valuable cargo rather than hang around. There was so much, of this illegal contraband, coming into our coastal beaches, that the occasional loss was considered to be an accepted part of that business. Another local guy, who I have recently met, told me that when he was in his early twenties he was rod fishing in some secluded inlet when he found a kilo of cocaine floating in some mangrove roots. He told me, without any apparent pangs of guilt, that he used half of his find for his own consumption. The other half he took by boat down to Jamaica and spent a month there while partying on the profit from the rest. A good number of people still hold the romantic view that these captains were sort of Robin Hood type characters who were robbing the rich and giving to the poor. I don't actually understand this but my lucky associate looks back on this occasion as one of the high lights of his life. A local fisherman who had friends in this illegal business, and was probably more involved than he would like to admit, has just released a book entitled "Marijuana Millionaires." This gives a more detailed and colorful sight into the inner workings of this risky yet profitable trade.

It seems somewhat strange, back in those days, that smoking marijuana was illegal and yet today it is now legal in almost half the States of the Union. My wife recently visited California and said that she could smell the faint sweet aroma of marijuana in virtually every public place that she visited in the Los Angles area. Even in today's States, where it is still illegal, petitions are being gathered to enact the legal use of this drug for purely medical purposes. People suffering from such maladies as multiple sclerosis, epilepsy and other similar afflictions, say that smoking marijuana gives them a modicum of pain relief. A similar petition, here in the State of Florida, just fail to be passed by a marginal amount and is due to be re-presented again soon and is expected to pass next time. In those States, where it is now legal, these businesses are thriving and their governments are reaping the benefits of the massive amounts of taxes raised by these sales. Another incremental benefit is that all these previous petty drug crimes have now been eliminated causing the jails and prisons to be less cluttered. Here again the governments, of these States, are saving millions of dollars due to this wind fall and these places of incarceration now have extra room to house the more hardened criminals. I guess it is an ill wind that does not blow good fortune to someone or other.

Even the Garden of Eden had its unpleasantness in the form of a serpant and here, on the one thousand mile tropical Florida coast line, we have the shark. Figures have just been released for 2015 and out of ninety eight, world wide attacks, thirty of them occurred here in Florida. This figure, believe it or not, is more than the combined total of Australia and South Africa which was merely twenty six. In Australia their major threat is the tiger shark, in South Africa it is the great white shark, while here in Florida the main culprit is the bull shark. The bull shark holds this unenviable title because it is capable of being able to swim in brakish waters thus making it to be the only shark able to thrive in river waters. In Florida a person must take great care when swimming, even if they are several miles inland, as this is still the territory of the bull shark and, unfortunately, this is where some attacks happen. Experts say that the increase in shark attacks is proportionate to the increased number of people who come to swim in the waters here. Since sharks mainly feed at night it is advisable not to swim, in their waters, between sun down and sun up. Most of attacks, here in Florida, happen on the east coast where the shark cannot clearly see through the sand laden Atlantic surf and thus mistakes human beings for seals or large fish. Also surf boarders are of special interest to sharks because again, from the sharks vantage point, beneath them, they

TELL IT LIKE IT IS

look very much like seals. In clear waters most sharks, during the day when not in a hunting mode, swim right past bathers without paying them any attention at all. However if you should find yourself in the water after dark, due of some unforeseen set of circumstances, make yourself as inconspicuous as possible by propelling yourself with the breast stroke. Do this calmly and quietly so as not to attract the shark's attention and with any amount of luck you might just stay alive.

CHAPTER TWENTY-FIVE

The Sweat Of Human Kindness

My wife and I have just returned from another memorable visit to the Florida Keys which, although is located the same State in which we live, somehow seems to be light years away. Sharon has a daughter who, with her husband, lives on Big Pine Key which is a little south of the famous Seven Mile Bridge. The journey is about four hundred miles and so if you average around sixty miles per hour it will take you approximately six and a half hours, by automobile, or seven hours assuming a stop for gas and food. On Friday we started our journey from Anna Maria Island direct to I 75 then straight south to Naples where we pick up Alligator Alley then across The Everglades to the outskirts of Fort Lauderdale. We then headed south down Chrome Road through Holmestead, to avoid the vast metropolis of Miami, and linked up with Highway One to Key Largo and on down the Keys. We passed through notable towns like Ilsa Mirada, known as one of the best fishing destinations in the Western Hemisphere and Marathon which is almost exactly half way down this string of isolated Keys. We left our home at around 9-00 AM and arrived in Marathon at mid afternoon.

156

One of the main reasons for making this trip was because Sharon's daughter, Danielle, was having some serious surgery and she was at the Fisherman's Hospital in Marathon. Sharon wanted to arrive before she was released and to stay with her for four or five days afterwards as she was recovering at home. So before going to our final destination, some twenty miles further south, Sharon wanted to stop at the hospital to see her. Because the ladies needed their privacy, to discuss the details of the surgery and the imminent regimen after her release, Sharon dropped me off at the Sunrise Grill right at the start of the Seven Mile Bridge. While there I had some cool cock-tails and good conversation with the locals until Sharon picked me back up to continue the last leg of our trek. My stop over was not too hard to endure since The Sunrise had its own swimming pool right next to the tiki bar where I had ensconced myself. It was easy for me to enjoy my visit there as everyone was sunning themselves or frolicking about in the water while immersing themselves in the typical laid back Florida Keys life style. After our intermission we drove the further twenty miles or so and arrived in time for dinner with Danielle's husband Lee who, like Danielle, is a Monroe County Sheriff and is also an aspiring chef. That night, the last before Danielle was released, we renewed our acquaintances with some of the local Moose members at their Lodge on Big Pine. The following day Danielle was released but while at home she was to be inactive, as her doctor had ordered, and so we stayed close at hand during the next four days.

There was a second pressing reason for us to make our trip, at this specific time, which was that a good friend of mine, back on Anna Maria Island, had entered to run in the Keys 100 Ultra-Marathon event. This unique race is, as the name suggest, a one hundred mile foot race from Key Largo to Key West and is the equivalent of four marathons. It is an annual run which is organized as a fund raising event to benefit prostrate cancer victims. There are various ways in which the competitors can participate and apart from the one hundred mile race there is a fifty mile run, from Marathon to Key West, a thirty mile run from Big Pine to Key West and there is also a six person, one hundred mile team relay race. These events all start at different times but they all end at Higgs Beach on Key West where a huge welcoming party is set up for them. My friend was due to begin his race at around 6-00 AM on the Saturday morning. Because he told me that he hoped to make the half way point at around 7-00 PM, that night, Sharon and I went to the fifty mile marker to greet him. We waited for two hours and at 9-00 PM, thinking that he had quit due to the heat and humidity, we left. We found out later that he passed that point one hour later, at 10-00 PM, as the grueling run had taken it's toll on his body. My gallant friend reluctantly quit around the sixty mile marker as his body, by this time, was wracked with pain and exhaustion. What an epic struggle to be out there, totally alone, when your body is screaming for you to quit but your mind is saying "don't stop!". Every one of these brave and dedicated runners should be commended for giving up their leisure time to participate in such a grueling yet magnificent venture.

The following day was Lee's last day off from work and, knowing that Danielle was being cared for, we drove down to the finishing line at Higgs Beach in Key West. A large marquee tent was set up with food and drinks being supplied to the runners and their supporters while the presentation of trophies was being made to all category winners. This was an uplifting experience but even more amazing was the fact that while all this was going on, stragglers were still staggering across the finish line to a tremendous roar of approval from the other jubilant contestants. Although they had no hope of any awards they still resolutely dragged their beaten bodies across that finish line. Some of them walked across, some limped across and some were carried across but I was moved by the fact that no matter how long it took to get there, somehow they got there. Being an athlete myself, in my younger years, I knew the dedication that it took to perform at this level and the fortitude that was needed to complete such an enormous undertaking. For the most part these were not dedicated athletes competing for fame or fortune, they were just strong willed, extraordinary people trying to help a good cause at the sacrifice of their own well being. Such heroism is rarely encountered outside of a military operation. When the first marathon was run it occurred when a runner had to report the victory, of his country, in a significant Greek battle. The legend also said that on reaching Marathon, and delivering his message, the brave runner dropped dead from exhaustion. All the participants, at whatever level in the Keys 100, should be proud of their achievements no matter how humble they consider them to be. Witnessing these stalwart people was indeed an inspiration and I will never be able to truly convey my admiration, of them, for their incredible endeavors.

When the Keys 100 beach party broke up Sharon and I went into Key West for a trip down memory lane. We went to Captain Tony's Bar one of our favorite and also one of the oldest watering holes in that town. On Duvall Street we sat, for a while, at The Bull and listened to some good music while watching the antics of the revelers passing by and chilled with some mighty fine beverages. As the evening began to draw in we gathered, with all that day's special event runners, at The Smoking Tuna and enjoyed every single war story about each competitors trials and tribulations.Apparently because of the excessive heat and hardship, throughout those two steamy days, all the times for each runner were slower than in previous years. The time for the winning runner, of the one hundred mile race, was almost four hours longer than the previous best. Out of the three hundred odd competitors who started the races around a third of them dropped out due to heat exhaustion. Others had to quit because of severe cramps, side stitches or badly blistered feet. Stories abounded concerning runners who had not an ounce of energy left as their stoic determination lapsed and had to be carried to waiting First Aid tents for medical treatment. This party was akin to a war veteran's gathering where each soldier compared his heroic deeds with his fellow combatants. The excitement was palpable and the comradeship was sincere and genuine with kudos being given to one and all. Before the night was through I heard people arranging to meet again next year and, believe it or not, do it all over again. In the words of Rudyard Kipling "You are a better man than I am Gunga Din!" On our last night we rounded off our trip with a visit to one of our favorite haunts called The No Name Pub and picked up some snazzy tee shirts which, I am sure, we will find a good reason to display them in public. Such is our Florida style of living.

In Summary

So there you have it, the always good, the not too bad and the never ugly. I hope that you have enjoyed this variegated view into the crevasses of my mind. I also hope that you have gleaned a modicum of new and useful information and found my views, here, to be be at least interesting if not thought provoking. I consider myself to be one of the luckiest people on planet Earth. When I think of just how my life might have been, I bless my good fortune and am proud of what I have managed to achieve. At my time of life I am where I want to be, doing what I want to do with the people that I am proud to be with. In my twilight years nothing can top that. Via con Dios, amigos.

Made in the USA
Charleston, SC
08 November 2016